PENGUIN CLASSICS

KING HARALD'S SAGA

SNORRI STURLUSON was born in 1179 and brought up at Oddi, the home of an aristocratic and cultured family in the south of Iceland (1181–1201). He then lived as a wealthy landowner, politician and lawyer, and was Lawspeaker of the Althing from 1215–18 and 1222–31. He visited Norway twice, 1218–20 (when he also went to Sweden) and 1237–9. In 1241 Snorri Sturluson was killed by his enemies. An outstanding personality of medieval Scandinavia and Iceland, he was the author of the *Edda*, a handbook of Scaldic art, *The Olaf Sagas*, probably of *Egil's Saga*, and of *Heimskringla*, a history of the kings of Norway from the half-mythical origins of the dynasty down to the year 1177.

MAGNUS MAGNUSSON is an Icelander who has been resident in Scotland for most of his life. After a career in newspaper journalism in Scotland, he is now a freelance author and broadcaster, best known as the presenter of the BBC quiz programme *Mastermind*. He is also chairman of the Scottish National Heritage. He studied English and Old Icelandic at Oxford University, and his hobby is translating from Icelandic, both old and new. With Hermann Pálsson he has translated three other Saga volumes for Penguin Classics, *Njal's Saga*, *Laxdæla Saga* and *The Vinland Sagas*.

HERMANN PÁLSSON studied Icelandic at the University of Iceland and Celtic at University College, Dublin. He was Professor in Icelandic at the University of Edinburgh, where he taught from 1950 to 1988. He was the General Editor of the New Saga Library and the author of many books on the history and literature of medieval Iceland; his more recent publications include *Legendary Fiction in Medieval Iceland* (with Paul Edwards), *Art and Ethics in Hrafnkel's Saga* and *Vikings in Russia* (with Paul Edwards). In addition to the three other Saga translations with Magnus Magnusson, Hermann Pálsson translated *Hrafnkel's Saga* and (with Paul Edwards) *Egil's Saga*, *Orkneyinga Saga*, *Eyrbyggja Saga* and *Seven Viking Romances* for Penguin Classics. He died in 2002.

SNORRI STURLUSON

King Harald's Saga

Harald Hardradi of Norway

Translated with an Introduction by
MAGNUS MAGNUSSON *and* HERMANN PÁLSSON

PENGUIN BOOKS

PENGUIN BOOKS

Published by the Penguin Group
Penguin Books Ltd, 80 Strand, London WC2R 0RL, England
Penguin Group (USA) Inc., 375 Hudson Street, New York, New York 10014, USA
Penguin Books Australia Ltd, 250 Camberwell Road, Camberwell, Victoria 3124, Australia
Penguin Books Canada Ltd, 10 Alcorn Avenue, Toronto, Ontario, Canada M4V 3B2
Penguin Books India (P) Ltd, 11 Community Centre, Panchsheel Park, New Delhi – 110 017, India
Penguin Group (NZ), cnr Airborne and Rosedale Roads, Albany, Auckland 1310, New Zealand
Penguin Books (South Africa) (Pty) Ltd, 24 Sturdee Avenue, Rosebank 2196, South Africa

Penguin Books Ltd, Registered Offices: 80 Strand, London WC2R 0RL, England

www.penguin.com

This translation first published 1966
Reprinted in Penguin Classics 2005

24

Copyright © Magnus Magnusson and Hermann Pálsson, 1966
All rights reserved

Printed in England by Clays Ltd, St Ives plc
Set in Linotype Pilgrim

ISBN-13: 978–0–140–44183–3

www.greenpenguin.co.uk

Penguin Books is committed to a sustainable future
for our business, our readers and our planet.
The book in your hands is made from paper
certified by the Forest Stewardship Council.

TO PROFESSOR SIGURÐUR NORDAL
on his eightieth birthday
14 September 1966

Contents

Introduction

THE year 1066 was a convulsive and fateful year for the destiny of England and western Europe. It was the year that brought together in violent and mortal conflict the three greatest military leaders in Europe of their day – Harald of Norway, Harold of England, and William of Normandy; three powerful and ambitious men who had fought their way to authority in their respective countries and who now, in three weeks of terrible bloodshed in the autumn of 1066, were to fight to the death for the greatest prize of all: the throne of England.

In Norway, King Harald Sigurdsson – Harald Hardradi, Harald the Ruthless, as later historians were to dub him – had fled into exile in 1030 at the age of fifteen when Norway was torn by civil war and his half-brother, King Olaf the Saint, was killed in battle by an army of his own rebellious subjects. After years of plundering in the Mediterranean and Asia Minor as a Viking mercenary in the service of the Byzantine emperors, Harald returned to claim the throne of Norway his brother had lost; and for the next twenty years he ruled Norway by iron discipline and force of arms, and terrorized neighbouring Denmark by constant raiding expeditions. By 1066 he was the most feared warrior in northern Europe, the last of the formidable Viking kings of Scandinavia; and at the age of fifty-one he embarked on the most ambitious enterprise of his relentless career – the conquest of England.

In France, Duke William of Normandy – William the Bastard as his contemporaries called him, William the Conqueror as he was to prove himself – had succeeded to a turbulent province as an illegitimate orphan at the age of seven, in 1035. His boyhood was a nightmare of treachery and danger; and even when he reached manhood he had to survive seven years of incessant warfare and rebellion between 1047 and 1054 before he was able to establish his authority over Normandy beyond serious dispute. By 1066, he was the battle-hardened leader of the most brilliant new secular and ecclesiastical aristocracy in Europe; and in his late thirties he was ready to claim by force what he regarded as a moral inheritance – the throne of England.

In England, Earl Harold Godwinsson – Harold of Wessex, later to become Harold II of England – was born into one of the most thrustful and ambitious family dynasties in Anglo-Saxon England. During the uneasy reign of Edward the Confessor (1042–66) he survived exile, and then returned to prove his military ability with crushing campaigns against the Welsh, and also his statesmanship by averting civil war between north and south over his brother, Earl Tostig. On 6 January 1066, at the age of forty-four, he was elected and crowned king of England – an England whose throne was threatened by rival claims from Scandinavia and Normandy, and weakened by lingering disaffection in the north. For the next nine months, Harold was busy organizing the nation's defences against the challenge he knew must come; what he could not know was from where it would come first.

In the event, it came from the north. In September 1066 Harald of Norway sailed across the North Sea with an invasion armada of over 300 ships and came prowling down the coast of Yorkshire. On 20 September, he landed his army of some 9,000 men and destroyed the northern army that barred his way to York at Fulford. But five days later, on Monday, 25 September, Harold of England arrived with another army after a forced march of 190 miles from London, and fell upon the surprised Norwegian invaders at Stamford Bridge. The slaughter that ensued was remembered with awe for generations; by nightfall, the Norwegian army was all but wiped out, and Harald of Norway lay dead. His death marked the end, to all intents and purposes, of the Viking era that so coloured the politics of medieval Europe, the end of 350 years, of Scandinavian harassment of England.

But when Harald of Norway died, his victor, Harold of England, himself had only nineteen more days to live. Three days after the Battle of Stamford Bridge, William of Normandy, descendant of the Viking invaders who had settled in France

150 years earlier, landed on the south coast of England with an army of 7,000 men; and Harold of England set off on a forced march once again, to fight the last battle to be fought on English soil against an invasion army, on the Downs above Hastings on 14 October 1066.

Just as the Battle of Stamford Bridge finally settled the Scandinavian threat, so the Battle of Hastings was to decide the fate and future destiny of Great Britain; and had it not been for the Norwegian invasion in the north of England some three weeks earlier, the Norman invasion in the south might well have ended very differently. In these three autumn weeks of 1066, the tension of the triangle formed by Norway, England, and Normandy, was decisively resolved. And it is one of the sides of that triangle – the conflict between Norway and England, between Viking Harald and Anglo-Saxon Harold – that forms the climax of *King Harald's Saga*.

*

King Harald's Saga is the biography of one of the most remarkable and memorable of the medieval kings of Norway; and it forms part of one of the most remarkable works of history to emerge from medieval Europe – *Heimskringla* ('The Orb of the World'), written some 170 years after the death of King Harald by the great Icelandic historian and saga-writer, Snorri Sturluson.

Heimskringla is truly an immense work, nothing more nor less than a complete history of Norway from prehistoric times down to 1177, told in a series of royal biographies of all the kings who occupied the throne of Norway. The vastness of its scope and conception is implicit in the very first words, the words that gave it its name – '*Heims kringla*, . . .' 'The orb of the world, on which mankind dwells. . .'. It starts far back in the remotest past, in a world of mythology peopled by shadowy legendary figures, the world of Odin and the Norse gods from whom sprang the royal house of Sweden and Norway (*Ynglinga Saga*); it continues through the semi-legendary decades of the ninth century, the era of Halfdan the Black, first of the Ynglings to establish royal authority in Norway (*Half-dan the Black's Saga*).

It is only with King Harald Fine-Hair, Halfdan's son, that history proper begins. He succeeded his father *c*. 860 at the age of ten, and it was he who unified all Norway under one crown during his long reign (he died in 933). It was during Harald's reign that Iceland was discovered and settled by the Norsemen, partly at least as a result of Harald's policy of subjugating all the independent chieftains to his authority : emigration became the only alternative to submission. The Icelandic historians who documented the history of Norway seem to have had extremely vague ideas about what happened in Norway before the settlement of Iceland (870–930); from then on, it is to the Icelanders, and particularly Snorri Sturluson, that we owe our detailed knowledge of the history of medieval Norway.

Snorri's great gallery of kings sweeps through the tenth century and culminates in the reign of King Olaf Tryggvason (995–1000), the iron king who forced many of the pagan Scandinavian lands to adopt Christianity. This completes the first section of *Heimskringla*.

The second section, which takes up about two fifths of the whole work, is a self-contained biography of King Olaf the Saint (1016–30), *St Olaf's Saga*. This work, in fact, was written first, as a separate saga-history, complete in itself, although it had an Introduction and Appendix summarizing Norway's history before and after St Olaf's reign, and these later formed the framework of sections I and III of *Heimskringla*. *St Olaf's Saga* is deservedly considered the greatest of the saga-histories in *Heimskringla*; and it was the model on which Snorri Sturluson based all his later historical writings.

After St Olaf's death in battle in 1030, section III of *Heimskringla* takes the history of Norway's kings onwards down to 1177, starting with the biography of King Magnus the Good, St Olaf's illegitimate son, who came to the throne in 1035. *King Magnus the Good's Saga* overlaps and merges into *King Harald's Saga*; and after King Harald's death at Stamford Bridge in 1066, Snorri takes the story on through the succession of kings who ruled Norway more or less effectively, more or less violently, for the next century, ending half-way through the reign of King Magnus Erlingsson (1161–84).

It is primarily the vastness of the conception of *Heimskringla*, the sweep and range of its scope, that marks it out from all the many other Icelandic saga-histories. There had been individual sagas before Snorri, and there were many after him; there had been synoptic histories and summaries before him; but no one, before or after, attempted anything on such a grand scale. A number of earlier historians had tackled individual kings and individual periods, using different sources; Snorri determined to synthesize the whole history of Norway.

Snorri Sturluson was essentially an explorer of the past. He did not allow himself to be deterred by the fact that the landmarks in the remotest area of history were so few and far between; where his information failed, he rationalized and deduced. When he emerged into the more familiar landscape of the late ninth century, he could build on the work of earlier historians, he could accept and reject, and add from sources of his own. But his primary purpose was not so much to correct earlier works of history, as to cultivate history for its own sake, to improve the *writing* of history; he wanted to illuminate the past, not merely to record it.

Snorri Sturluson has always been the most celebrated figure in Icelandic literature (principally, perhaps, because so few of the saga-authors are now known by name), and *Heimskringla*, particularly abroad, has remained the best-known of all the major works in Icelandic saga literature; it was the first saga work to be printed (in a summary in a Danish translation in 1594). In Norway especially, its popularity and influence have been enormous, and it was a potent factor in awakening Norway's desire for independence in the nineteenth century, by reminding Norwegians of their heroic past.

And yet *Heimskringla* is not a work of history at all, in the modern sense of the term. It is a series of *saga*-histories – and the distinction is a vital one. Snorri Sturluson saw history as a continual flow, and in *Heimskringla* he tried to convey this to his readers; but it was not so much a matter of historical evolution as a long chain of events, and these events he saw in terms, almost exclusively, of individual personalities. He saw politics in terms of personal motivation, of human aspirations and failings. *Heimskringla* is a composite, a portrait gallery of these individuals; and each individual king's saga is conceived partly as a self-contained entity and partly as a link in this chain of events.

In the past, *Heimskringla* has been accepted, uncritically, as the gospel of Scandinavian history, as unassailable as Holy Writ. Modern scholarship, however, has shown how misleading this view has been; yet this has by no means diminished the importance of *Heimskringla*. Indeed, by putting its historical value into truer perspective, we can now concentrate more attention on Snorri Sturluson's artistry as a saga-writer. The great Family Sagas of Iceland, like *Njal's Saga* or *Egil's Saga* or *Laxdœla Saga*, were more concerned with the character and fate of individuals than with strict historical accuracy; historical truth and plausible fiction were often so thoroughly fused that it is hardly possible to separate the one from the other.

Precisely the same is true of the History Sagas. The historical facts, so far as they were known, were used chiefly to portray the personalities and characters involved in them. The 'success' of a saga does not depend on its historical accuracy so much as on the skill with which its individual characters are portrayed, and Snorri Sturluson's greatest achievement, perhaps, was to have created such an immense gallery of brilliantly executed royal portraits from the past. The Harald of *King Harald's Saga* is one of the most impressive of these portraits; but fascinating and convincing as he appears in Snorri's pages, he may have been a very different person in real life. Even where we know, from a comparison with other sources (especially English sources where events in England in 1066 are concerned), that Snorri Sturluson's facts are considerably inaccurate, his account is always eminently plausible.

Although part of Snorri's purpose was to preserve for posterity a truthful account of past events, he was also guided by aesthetic principles; above all, he was trying to create a work of literature, and it is essential to distinguish the literary and historical aspects if we are to understand and evaluate *King Harald's Saga* properly. In Snorri Sturluson's case, we are fortunate in that we know so much about the author; for all the Icelandic saga-histories were created by individual writers who had their own reasons for treating their subject-matter in the particular way they did, and who were writing for a particular audience. Snorri Sturluson's life and times are extremely relevant to any interpretation of the sagas he wrote.

*

Had Snorri Sturluson lived in an earlier age, he would undoubtedly have had a saga written about him, instead of being a saga-writer himself. For he lived at a critical time in the history of Iceland, when the unique parliamentary commonwealth established in 930 was disintegrating in a welter of power struggles between half a dozen ruling families who competed savagely for power and wealth, and Iceland itself was being irresistibly drawn into the ambit of the Norwegian crown once more; and Snorri himself was one of the leading political figures in this story of progressive disintegration until national independence was eventually lost in 1262.

His life was just as extraordinary and full of drama as any of the Norwegian kings he depicted in *Heimskringla*, his own character just as complex and ambiguous. He was a man of astonishing contradictions: a man who fought and schemed all his life to become the most powerful chieftain in Iceland, yet who still found time to write some of the greatest masterpieces in Icelandic literature; a greedy, covetous man who was none the less capable of great generosity; a patriot so fascinated by the royal court of Norway that he could harbour secret thoughts of treason; a farmer who wanted to be an aristocrat, a prose-writer who wanted to be a poet, a scholar who cared more about owning property; a worldly, cultivated man who loved all the good things of life – wealth, women, wine, good company – yet who died a squalid, tragic death in the cellar of his own home.

He was born to wealth and authority in 1179 at Hvamm, an estate in the west of Iceland, a descendant of some of the greatest and most talented figures in Iceland's early history. On his father's side he was descended from influential chieftains like Snorri the Priest (d. 1031), whose son Halldor Snorrason fought at the side of King Harald Sigurdsson of Norway (cf. *King Harald's Saga*), and from Gudmund the Powerful, another of Iceland's leading chieftains, who figures prominently in many of the Icelandic Sagas, including *Njal's Saga*.

On his mother's side, he was descended from Markus Skegg-jason, poet and Law-Speaker to the Icelandic Althing (d. 1107), and from the great Icelandic viking-poet, Egil Skalla-Grimsson, eponymous hero of *Egil's Saga* (which many scholars are convinced was written by Snorri Sturluson himself).

His life was to be conditioned by the traits he inherited: the sense of grandeur, of dynastic pride, of political destiny – and the artistic creativeness. And it was to be shaped, too, by his upbringing; for at the age of two, in 1181, Snorri was sent to be fostered at Oddi, the outstanding centre of culture and learning in Iceland at that time, the home of the most culti-vated chieftain in the country, Jon Loptsson (1124–97). It was here that Snorri was to come into close contact with the writing of history, and particularly with the royal court of Norway; for Jon Loptsson was the grandson of the first Ice-landic historian, Sæmund Sigfusson the Learned (1056–1133), who was educated in France and who wrote a Latin summary (now lost) of the history of the kings of Norway.

But more importantly, Jon Loptsson was the grandson of King Magnus Bare-Legs of Norway, that violent man who reigned for a lurid decade between 1093 and 1103 and who died at the age of thirty on a military expedition in Ireland. Jon Loptsson's mother, Thora, was one of King Magnus's ille-gitimate children, and the men of Oddi were inordinately proud of the fact. So proud were they that a eulogy was com-posed in honour of Jon Loptsson round about the year 1190 (when Snorri was about eleven years old), tracing his descent right down through the royal house of Norway from King Halfdan the Black. This poem, *Noregs Konunga Tal* ('List of Norwegian Kings'), which is eighty-three strophes long, is in effect a summarized history of Norway.

Jon Loptsson himself had been fostered in Norway, and had attended many state occasions there. So young Snorri Sturluson was reared on a diet of learning and scholarship, with particular reference to the royal house of Norway. At Oddi he had access to the Icelandic saga and historical literature that was slowly accumulating throughout the twelfth century; but he was also gaining experience of the royal courts of Scandinavia, which were later to play such a significant part in his life.

After Jon Loptsson's death in 1197, Snorri immediately threw himself zealously into the pursuit of power and position. He married into money, and thereby inherited the estate of Borg, which had been the home of his ancestor Egil Skalla-Grimsson. A few years later he moved to Reykholt, an estate in Borgarfjord in the west of Iceland, which seems to have been a seat of learning even before Snorri's time and was now to be his home for the rest of his life.

In the first two decades of the thirteenth century, Snorri Sturluson quickly pushed himself to the forefront of national life in Iceland. He was amassing wealth and power, and soon owned vast estates and lands in many parts of the country by taking over the chieftaincies into which Iceland had originally been divided. His life was an intricate pattern of shifting alliances and friendships, and in 1215, at the age of thirty-six, he was elected to his first three-year period as Law-Speaker of the Althing (he was to serve as Law-Speaker again, from 1222 to 1231). His chief literary interest during this period was not prose but poetry; he was already well known as a poet, writing in the sophisticated but dying art of the so-called court-metre, the style used by all the Icelanders who had become professional Court Poets to the royal courts of Scandinavia. But as well as writing poetry, he was collecting it assiduously; when he came to write his history-sagas, it was his prodigious stock of re-membered Court Poetry on which he drew as one of his chief sources of historical material.

In 1218 he paid his first visit to Scandinavia. He stayed at the court of King Hakon Hakonsson, that shrewd and wily king who eventually succeeded in annexing Iceland to the Nor-wegian throne, in 1262, and who died in Orkney the following year after his campaign against Scotland had been foiled at the Battle of Largs in 1263. Snorri also visited Sweden, where he was given an honoured reception at the court of the late Earl Hakon the Mad, in whose honour he had already composed a poem for which he had received handsome gifts (he now wrote another poem, in honour of the widow, entitled *Andvaka* – 'Sleeplessness').

Snorri's first visit to Scandinavia was in every way a triumph. He was held in high esteem at the Norwegian court, and was appointed a gentleman-in-waiting. He was an undoubted favourite with young King Hakon and his regent and mentor, Duke Skuli. And on his return to Iceland, he thanked his patrons by composing in their honour a poem of 102 strophes, *Háttatal* ('List of Metres'), a *tour de force* of technical proficiency, illustrating the various court-metres. This poem formed the final section of Snorri Sturluson's first major work, the *Prose Edda*, a textbook of poetry and poetic diction whose lavish examples have preserved for us a great deal of information about early Norse mythology and heroic legend.

He was not to return to Norway for fifteen years – and then it was to be in rather different circumstances. During this intervening period, Snorri was engaged in an incredible series of feuds and intrigues, sometimes against members of his own family. The Icelandic republic was now entering the start of its death throes, and Snorri's family was to lend its own name to this era – the Sturlung Age, an age of flagrant lawlessness, of pledges broken and honour cynically ignored, of pitched battles between chieftains and their changing supporters, of cruelty and treachery and arson and murder.

And all the while, King Hakon in Norway watched and waited, playing off one chieftain against another, only awaiting his opportunity to step in decisively when the nation had become exhausted by this savage civil strife. Like most of the other leading men in Iceland, Snorri Sturluson was drawn helplessly into this political vortex; the dark forces of self-destruction had got out of hand and the state was doomed.

And yet, throughout this period of intrigue and slaughter, somehow Snorri Sturluson found time to write, to dictate to his secretary in the privacy of his library a steady stream of sagas. We cannot now be sure exactly what he wrote; the sixteenth-century *Annals of Oddi* say of him, laconically, 'He composed Edda and many other books of learning, Icelandic sagas.' His nephew, the writer Sturla Thordarson (1214–84), wrote in his *Íslendinga Saga* ('Saga of the Icelanders') that in the winter of 1230–1, another of Snorri's nephews, Sturla Sighvatsson, 'spent a long time at Reykholt and paid much attention to having books of sagas written up from the books which Snorri had composed'.

Hindsight casts an almost wistful light on this peaceful winter of 1230–1, when this great man of letters entertained his nephew and the talk was all of saga-writing; for within a very few years the same nephew, Sturla Sighvatsson, had become King Hakon's agent and was determined to gain supreme power for himself, even at his uncle's expense. Snorri was now in considerable danger, and in 1237 he prudently went abroad; he was no longer the high favourite he had once been, at least not with King Hakon. Hakon's former regent, Duke Skuli, was now at odds with the king, and it was with Duke Skuli that Snorri took refuge.

In Iceland, the balance of power had shifted once again. Snorri's nephew, Sturla Sighvatsson, who had been threatening Snorri's very life, had himself been killed by yet another contender for supreme power – Gissur Thorvaldsson, another of King Hakon's agents.

In 1239, Snorri decided to return to Iceland. King Hakon banned all Icelanders from leaving Norway, but Snorri left none the less, bearing with him the title – the empty title – of 'Earl' bestowed on him by the discredited Earl Skuli. Snorri Sturluson was now a spent force in Icelandic politics, little capable of either helping or hindering the king's cause, or of proving a stumbling-block to Gissur Thorvaldsson's ambitions; but Gissur was determined to smash the powerful Sturlung family for good.

Gissur's excuse came with a letter from King Hakon demanding that Snorri Sturluson should be brought to Norway – or killed if he refused to go. Snorri was never to be given the

option. On the night of 23 September 1241, seventy un-
announced visitors led by Gissur Thorvaldsson arrived at
Reykholt. The house was unguarded. They went unchallenged
through the sturdy stockade that Snorri had built around the
farmhouse for just such an emergency, and then forced their
way into the house. Snorri was asleep in his bed-closet, but
managed to get away as they were breaking into it. Eventually
they found him hiding in a cellar underneath the buildings.
Five men went down into the cellar; and there, unarmed and
defenceless, Iceland's most distinguished man of letters was
struck down and killed. He was sixty-two years old.

*

The manner of Snorri Sturluson's death still has the power to
shock, even seven centuries after the event – that a man of
such outstanding literary gifts should be slaughtered so brutally,
and to such little purpose. Yet it is arguable that had Snorri
not been so deeply involved in the power-politics of his age
(and paid the price for that involvement), he would never have
achieved the kind of insight and experience that informs his
work as a saga-historian. Had he not been Snorri Sturluson the
chieftain, would he ever have been Snorri Sturluson the writer?
He was essentially a man of his age; and his attitude to kingship, to power, to politics, was conditioned by his own experience of them. As a historian, as a saga-writer, he was using
the thirteenth-century present, as he alone could know it, to
illuminate the past.

He was also a man of his age in his literary philosophy, in
his theories of literary craftsmanship. Behind Snorri Sturluson
lay a century of saga-writing in Iceland, covering a wide
variety of subjects in a considerable diversity of styles. The
Danish historian, Saxo Grammaticus (d. 1216), writing his Latin
Gesta Danorum at the end of the twelfth century, acknowledged his debt to the Icelandic historians and saga-writers with
this tribute:

> The Icelanders . . . take great pleasure in learning and recording
> the history of all peoples, and they consider it just as meritorious to
> describe the exploits of others as to perform them themselves.

Snorri Sturluson had a considerable body of historical work to build on, stretching back a century to the works of Ari Thorgilsson the Learned (1067–1148), whom Snorri singled out for praise in his Introduction to *Heimskringla*:

I think his history altogether remarkable; he was very understanding, and he was so old that he had been born in the year after King Harald Sigurdsson's death. . . . It is not surprising that Ari knew the truth about events of the past both here and abroad, for he had got his information from old and wise men, and he himself was eager to learn and had a good memory.

Ari was a meticulous and scrupulous historian, a man who was careful to weigh all his sources and reject whatever he could not accept as fully accurate; he ended his Prologue to his *Íslendingabók* ('Book of Icelanders' – the only one of his works that now survives in its original form) with the words that should be every historian's motto: 'But if anything is misstated in this book, one should prefer whatever proves to be more accurate.'

Snorri Sturluson echoes this pious objectivity in a passage in *King Harald's Saga* itself (chapter 36) – although one cannot help feeling that, a century later, it was more a matter of perfunctory lip-service to a traditional ideal:

But many more of his [King Harald's] feats and achievements have not been written about here, partly because of our lack of knowledge, and partly because we are reluctant to place on record stories that are unsubstantiated. Although we have been told various stories and have heard about other deeds, it seems to us better that our account should later be expanded than that it should have to be emended.

By the time that Snorri Sturluson was writing, saga-history had developed a long way from Ari's method. Yet Ari had been much more than a mere annalist or chronicler; for when, in *Íslendingabók*, he came to what was to him, as a priest, the kernel of Iceland's history – the conversion to Christianity in the year 1000 – he broke into a superbly dramatic narrative, bringing vividly to life all the tensions and strife at the Althing that year when pagans and Christians were on the brink of civil war and one man was entrusted with the fateful decision about which religion the nation should adopt. This was saga-history as opposed to 'pure' history; this was the narrative craft that was to fertilize the great achievements of the thirteenth-century saga-writers.

Not surprisingly, it found its best expression in sagas about contemporary events. Snorri Sturluson occasionally cites as one of his sources a lost work called *Hryggjarstykki* ('Backbone-piece'), written early in the second half of the twelfth century by an Icelander called Eirik Oddsson. This seems to have been a contemporary history of Norway's twelfth-century kings, and it is the contemporaneity that Snorri quotes with approval :

Eirik was an intelligent man, and spent a long time in Norway during this period. He wrote a part of this story according to information given to him by Hakon Magi (Hakon and his sons were involved in all these disputes and schemes). Eirik also names other knowledgeable and reliable men who told him about these events, men who were present to see or hear what happened. . . .

The ultimate in this development, before Snorri's time, was *King Sverrir's Saga*, the biography of King Sverrir of Norway (1184–1201). It was written by an Icelandic priest, Karl Jonsson (d. 1212), abbot of the Benedictine monastery of Thingeyrar. Abbot Karl knew King Sverrir well, and stayed with him in Norway from 1185 to 1190; and when he wrote his friend's biography, King Sverrir himself was the chief source for the work and advised Abbot Karl what he should write and how he should write it. It is for this reason that Snorri Sturluson ended his *Heimskringla* at the year 1177 – the year at which *King Sverrir's Saga* begins – because Snorri felt there was nothing he could add to Abbot Karl's work.

But there was another stream of saga-history developing at the monastery at Thingeyrar and elsewhere in Iceland at this time – the writing of hagiographic biography. Two of Norway's kings in particular were singled out for this attention. Two monks, first Odd Snorrason and then Gunnlaug Leifsson, were engaged in writing biographies, in Latin, of King Olaf Tryggvason (995–1000), whom they regarded as the evangelist of Iceland and wanted to see canonized as Iceland's national saint.

The inspiration for these pious compositions was undoubtedly an earlier biography of St Olaf (1016–30), whose cult had spread rapidly all over Europe after his death at the Battle of Stiklestad. In these hagiographic sagas, miracle-tales and improbable legends were used quite uncritically. A later version of *St Olaf's Saga* was compiled by Snorri Sturluson's contemporary and close friend, Styrmir Karason the Learned (d. 1245), in which there was only the most perfunctory attempt at historicity; in his Epilogue, Styrmir wrote,

You can accept from this composed saga whatever you think most likely, for in old sagas many things are confused. This is only to be expected where oral tradition alone supplies the material. . . .

When Snorri Sturluson turned his hand to the writing of saga-histories, first with his own *St Olaf's Saga* and then with the first and third sections of *Heimskringla*, he was faced with the problem of writing about the past in the style of the contemporary biographers, but without the advantage of their first-hand source material.

In his Introduction to *Heimskringla*, Snorri records how he shaped his sources about the prehistory of Norway :

In this book, I have had written [a reference to his use of an amanuensis, this] old stories about the rulers who have had kingdoms in Scandinavia and who spoke the Danish tongue, according to how I have heard learned men tell them; also, some of their family trees, as I myself have been taught them. Some of this is to be found in the genealogies in which kings and other men of distinguished birth have traced their descent; but some of it is written according to old poems or historical lays, which people have used to entertain themselves with. And although we do not know the truth of them, we do, however, know of examples when old and learned men have reckoned them to be true.

There is no explicit claim to historical accuracy in that cautiously worded passage; instead, there is a distinction drawn between the entertainment value of some stories, as opposed to their historical accuracy.

When he came to the period from King Harald Fine-Hair (860–930) onwards, Snorri was just as cautious. Modern scholarship has now been able to analyse Snorri's many written sources and his use of them fairly comprehensively; but only Ari Thorgilsson is singled out for mention by Snorri himself in his Introduction to *Heimskringla* – no doubt because Ari was the only historian he could trust unreservedly, and because Ari by that time had an unassailable reputation in Iceland as a reliable authority.

There is no need here to enumerate all the written sources which Snorri is known to have used for *Heimskringla*. For *King Harald's Saga* in particular, Snorri is known to have used at least three basic written sources which are still extant: *Ágrip* ('Summary of the History of the Kings of Norway'), which is a brief history of Norway's kings from the ninth century to the twelfth, probably written before the end of the twelfth century by an Icelander living in Norway; *Morkinskinna* ('Mouldy Vellum'), compiled early in the thirteenth century, a composite of sagas of individual kings from the death of St Olaf (1030) to the twelfth century; and *Fagurskinna* ('Handsome Vellum'), a similar kind of compilation made a few years later by an Icelander living in Norway.

Close examination of these sources and comparison with Snorri's text by scholars like Professor Sigurður Nordal have revealed clearly how eclectic and selective Snorri Sturluson was as a historian.

But the material in which Snorri placed most faith as a source of historical information was the vast corpus of Court Poetry composed by the Icelanders who had monopolized the posts of Court Poets in Scandinavia and farther afield since the tenth century. In his Introduction, Snorri wrote:

When Harald Fine-Hair was king of Norway, Iceland was settled. With Harald there were Court Poets, and even now their poems are known, as well as the poems about all the kings who have reigned in Norway since then. And the best evidence we have is that which is contained in the poems which were composed for the kings themselves or their sons. We accept as true everything which is to be found in these poems concerning their journeyings or their battles.

It is, of course, the way of Court Poets to lavish the most praise on the people for whom the poems were composed; but no one would dare to tell the king himself about deeds which everyone present, including the king, would know to be nonsense and lies: that would be mockery, not praise. . . .

Thus, at a crucial point in *King Harald's Saga*, where Harald is said to have been the man who blinded the Byzantine emperor (chapter 14), Snorri cites two appropriate verses and underlines his faith in them as a source:

In these two eulogies in honour of Harald, as well as in many other poems about him, it is stated that Harald himself blinded the Byzantine emperor. The poets would surely have attributed this act to a duke or count or some other man of rank if they had known that to be true; but this was the account brought back by Harald himself and the men who were with him.

A Court Poet, in effect, could over-praise; but he could not lie.

So Snorri concludes his Introduction to *Heimskringla*, after praising Ari Thorgilsson for his historical accuracy and the validity of his sources, by reiterating his faith in Court Poetry:

But the poems, I think, are the least liable to be distorted, if they are correctly composed and sensibly interpreted.

Court Poetry was an intensely esoteric and sophisticated art-form, as complex in shape as an acrostic, and its intricate forms made considerable demands on the poet as well as on the audience. It is clear that most of the Icelandic scribes who copied out the Court Poetry in manuscripts of the later Middle Ages often did not fully understand what it meant. But if the poem were 'correctly composed', if the alliteration and internal assonance and syllabic metre were technically correct, the complicated form of the poem meant that it could be remembered and recited correctly even though the actual meaning had become obscure; it was then up to the historian to ensure that it was 'sensibly interpreted'. Snorri Sturluson, who must have made a lifelong study of Court Poetry and had already written a poetry textbook, the *Prose Edda*, used this source more liberally and with greater understanding than any other Icelandic historian.

It is this liberal use of Court Poetry that gives such a distinctive flavour to *King Harald's Saga* and the rest of *Heimskringla*. There are no fewer than ninety-one stanzas, culled from the work of twelve poets, studding the narrative of *King Harald's Saga*, and he used them as the historical kernel, as evidence of the 'journeyings and battles' he referred to in his Introduction; they created the framework which he fleshed out with traditional accounts, both oral and written, and his own interpretations.

Snorri wrote in *King Harald's Saga* (chapter 36):

A great deal of information about King Harald is contained in the poems which Icelandic poets presented to him and his sons; and because of his interest in poetry, he was a great friend of theirs.

Snorri might have added that because of Harald's generosity, the poets were great friends of his, too; indeed, he quotes a half-strophe by King Harald's favourite Court Poet, Thjodolf Arnorsson, which praises the king's generosity to his poets (chapter 99).

For Snorri, as a Court Poet himself and a close student of Court Poetry, understood the essential relationship between a king and his poets. Basically, it was a strict business relationship; the Icelandic Court Poets were professionals who sold their eulogies to foreign monarchs wherever the Norse tongue was spoken and this *genre* of poetry appreciated. They did not necessarily owe any personal allegiance to the kings they praised; indeed, one of the most remarkable Court Poems ever written in Icelandic, by Snorri Sturluson's great ancestor, Egil Skalla-Grimsson, was a eulogy composed in honour of his most bitter enemy – Eirik Blood-Axe. On that occasion, in York c. 950, Egil composed for Eirik Blood-Axe the poem *Head-Ransom* on the eve of his execution – not for payment in gold but, as the title indicates, for his head; and Eirik was so impressed with it that he granted Egil his life.

Snorri was well aware of the poetic conventions – that all kings, whoever they were, had to be called brave, gallant in battle, scourges of their enemies, etc. But he could also tell the merely conventional; for he knew that some poets – and usually the best ones – often became inseparably attached to

26

their kings, giving them an emotional allegiance and sometimes choosing to die by their side, as Thjodolf Arnorsson became attached to King Harald and as many of St Olaf's greatest poets did.

The kings used their poets deliberately as royal annalists, and royal propagandists. Snorri tells a story in his *St Olaf's Saga* to illustrate this: just before his last battle at Stiklestad, St Olaf summoned his Court Poets into his shield-rampart and said to them:

You are to stay here and see what happens; then you will not need others to tell you of it later, for you can tell the story and make verses about it yourselves afterwards.

Throughout *Heimskringla*, Snorri is careful to make a distinction between poems composed some time after the event, and poems composed at the time by eyewitnesses; in *King Harald's Saga*, the retrospective account is always introduced by the phrase 'In the words of the poet. . .', in contrast to the on-the-spot account which is prefaced by the words 'Then the poet said. . .'. But despite Snorri's manifest care, there are times in the saga when his poetry sources have misled him, however 'correctly composed and sensibly interpreted' they were. Sometimes the 'journeyings and battles' came adrift from their context and were misapplied; for instance, the verses about Earl Waltheof and his resistance to William of Normandy, attributed to the poet Thorkel Skallason and cited in chapters 96 and 97, seem to have referred to Waltheof's uprising in 1069 and not, as Snorri thought, to the Battle of Hastings. And it is ironic that although Snorri confidently cites the authority of Court Poets for the fact that Harald blinded the Byzantine emperor (chapter 14), Greek sources prove conclusively that Snorri made Harald blind the *wrong* emperor.

Apart from these main sources – earlier written histories, and Court Poetry – Snorri Sturluson had one other source of material at his disposal – oral traditions. It is very hard to form any kind of accurate assessment of the value Snorri placed on these. By the thirteenth century, there cannot have been very many ungarbled oral traditions left that earlier historians had not used or rejected; and Snorri's references to Ari Thorgilsson in his Introduction to *Heimskringla* stress the great age of his informants, and the long span of years their memories could cover. However Snorri also seems to have used his time in Norway and Sweden to collect oral traditions, and to visit the burial mounds of many of the earlier kings and other historic sites to gain information for himself. Snorri's foster-father, Jon Loptsson, was very knowledgeable about twelfth-century Norwegian affairs, and will have told Snorri of events which he himself had witnessed in Norway. More significantly, perhaps, Snorri's own ancestor, Halldor Snorrason, was one of King Harald's close companions during his years as a Varangian mercenary in the Mediterranean; and it is more than likely that family traditions about King Harald were handed down from generation to generation, and that these helped to shape Snorri's portrait of this remarkable warrior-king of Norway.

*

There is one further factor that should be borne in mind when one tries to assess Snorri Sturluson's methods and achievement in his portrayal of King Harald Sigurdsson – and that is the audience for whom he was writing. We know of one saga-history at least, written in the second half of the thirteenth century, which was specifically commissioned by a king of Norway – the biography of King Hakon Hakonsson, *King Hakon's Saga*, commissioned the year after King Hakon's death in 1263 by his son, King Magnus Hakonsson, from Snorri Sturluson's nephew, Sturla Thordarson. It has also been suggested that *King Sverrir's Saga* (see above, p. 22) was commissioned from Abbot Karl Jonsson by King Sverrir himself; and although there is no evidence to support this directly, King Sverrir undoubtedly had a hand in shaping its narrative.

In Snorri Sturluson's case, there can be no doubt whatsoever that *Heimskringla* was written not for a Norwegian audience, but an Icelandic one, although in his Prologue to *St Olaf's Saga* Snorri also recognizes the possibility that his work might find its way abroad:

I realize that if this account should reach other countries, it will be thought that I have spoken rather too much about Icelanders;

but the reason for this is the fact that the Icelanders who witnessed the events or heard about them, brought to this country the stories which later generations have since learned.

Presumably, Snorri must have hoped that *Heimskringla* would reach a wider public – what author does not? But because it was primarily intended for Icelandic audiences, it should be remembered that Snorri's viewpoint and sympathies did not necessarily coincide with Norwegian ideas. Norway, after all, was a foreign country, and an Icelander was quite capable of sympathizing with Norway's enemies.

To the early Norwegian historians, like the monk Theodoricus (*Historia de antiquitate regum Norwagiensium, c.* 1180), King Harald was a model king, described as being powerful, sagacious, brave in battle, steadfast, and ambitious. In some of the early Icelandic histories, it is King Harald's kindness and fairness and sense of humour that are emphasized – no doubt because, as Snorri states (chapter 36), King Harald seems to have treated Iceland sympathetically. To the Danish-inspired historians, however, King Harald was the embodiment of all evil – not surprisingly, considering how severely Denmark suffered from his constant attacks. The German monk Adam of Bremen, writing his history of the archbishopric of Hamburg less than a decade after Harald's death (*Gesta Hammaburgensis Ecclesiae Pontificum, c.* 1072), gained most of his information about Scandinavia from Harald's arch-enemy, King Svein Ulfsson of Denmark, and Harald appears in his pages as the devil incarnate; and some later historians even accused him of having murdered his own brother, St Olaf.

(This is certainly more in keeping with King Harald's familiar nickname, Harald the Ruthless; but the sobriquet *Harðráði* was never used by the early historians, and it first appeared only in occasional chapter-headings in manuscript copies dating from the thirteenth century.)

Snorri Sturluson's approach to the portrayal of King Harald was at once more objective and much more personal; it cannot be stressed too often that *King Harald's Saga* is essentially one individual writer's interpretation of King Harald and of certain personality conflicts during his reign.

In *King Harald's Saga*, Snorri Sturluson wrote in his 'obituary' of King Harald (chapter 99):

We have no particular accounts about his youth until the age of fifteen, when he took part in the Battle of Stiklestad with his brother, King Olaf the Saint.

And it was at that point in Harald's career that Snorri opened the saga.

But in fact, Snorri *did* have two stories about Harald before the saga opens, stories which he had already recounted in *St Olaf's Saga*. And these are of crucial importance to our understanding of King Harald the man; if the child really is father to the man, as the proverb has it, no man ever lived up to his childhood better than Harald. This is how Snorri told the story in *St Olaf's Saga*, chapter 76:

It is said that once when King Olaf was at a feast given by his mother, Queen Asta, she led forward her children and showed them to him. King Olaf put his half-brother Guthorm on one knee, and Halfdan on the other. He looked at the two boys, and then pulled a face and scowled at them, until the two boys were on the point of crying. Queen Asta then brought in her youngest son, who was called Harald; he was three years old then. The king pulled a face at him too, but the boy only stared back at him. Then the king took told of the boy's hair and pulled it; the boy thereupon took hold of the king's moustache, and gave it a tug in return.

King Olaf said, 'You're going to be vengeful one day, kinsman.'

Next day the king went out for a walk through the township with his mother Asta, and they came to a pond where the two boys, Guthorm and Halfdan, were playing together. In their game, they had huge farms with large barns, and big herds of cattle and sheep.

Young Harald was playing by himself some distance away at the pond-side, where there was a muddy creek; he had a number of wooden chips floating on the water. The king asked him what they were. Harald said they were his warships. King Olaf laughed and said, 'The time may well come, one day, when you will be in command of warships.'

Then King Olaf called Guthorm and Halfdan over to him.

'What would *you* like to have most of, Guthorm?' he asked.

'Corn-fields,' said the boy.

'How big a corn-field would you like to own?' asked the king.

'I want the whole headland jutting into the lake to be sown with corn every summer,' said Guthorm. There were ten farms on that headland.

'A great deal of corn could be grown there,' agreed King Olaf.

Then he asked Halfdan what *he* would like most of.

'Cattle,' said Halfdan.

'How many cattle would you like to own?' asked the king.

'So many,' said Guthorm, 'that when they came down to the water to drink, they would stand shoulder to shoulder right round the whole lake.'

'You want a big farm,' said the king. 'How like your father!'

Then King Olaf said to Harald, 'What would *you* like to own most of?'

'Warriors,' said Harald.

'How many would you like to have?'

'So many,' said Harald, 'that they would eat all Halfdan's cattle in one meal.'

The king laughed and turned to Asta. 'That's a king you're bringing up, mother!' said King Olaf.

It is not unlikely that Snorri Sturluson wrote that episode in *St Olaf's Saga* a good ten years before he began to write *King Harald's Saga*; yet there, in one brilliantly visualized episode, the future character and career of Harald Sigurdsson were outlined in all their essentials.

The other revealing episode about young Harald that Snorri relates in *St Olaf's Saga* comes just before the fateful Battle of Stiklestad (chapter 209):

King Olaf said, 'I think it better that my brother should not take part in the battle, for he is still only a child.'

'I shall certainly take part in the battle,' said Harald. 'And if I am too weak to grip the sword, I know what to do – I shall tie my hand to the hilt. There is no one more eager than I to cause trouble for these farmers. I intend to be with my men.'

These two episodes form a preface to a biography which in Snorri's hands becomes the story of a warrior's progress. Essentially it is the life and career of a professional soldier, starting with a battle – the Battle of Stiklestad, where Harald, aged fifteen, is wounded and his brother the king killed – and ending in battle, thirty-six years later at Stamford Bridge; a rounded, superbly told story of constant strife and struggle, bracketed at beginning and end with violence.

Right away, in the first chapter, we get one flashing glimpse of Harald's character, an echo of the three-year-old boy with warlike ambitions. After the disastrous Battle of Stiklestad, Harald is fleeing from his native country, a fugitive in disguise, escorted by a peasant who does not even know his identity; and Harald muses to himself in a thoughtful couplet,

'Who knows, my name may yet become
Renowned far and wide in the end.'

The lust for fame, for renown, is sharply revealed as one of the driving forces of his personality. The whole of the rest of his life is seen as his attempt to satisfy this driving force, to fulfil himself. Everything he does thereafter is bent towards this aim: his savage plundering in the Mediterranean has only one purpose, to achieve fame and status for himself and to amass enough treasure to finance his eventual struggle for power in Norway.

Having achieved authority in Norway, King Harald takes care to employ numerous Court Poets to keep his fame alive. Ambition and greed form the mainspring of his violent life; whenever his position is threatened, he resorts to any kind of treachery to safeguard it. In Snorri's interpretation, King Harald overwinds that spring when he attempts the conquest of England – and the spring that was wound up at the Battle of Stiklestad in chapter 1 snaps at Stamford Bridge.

But the interpretation is never made explicit – that was not the style of the saga-writers. It is only at the end of the saga that there is a formal 'appreciation' and description, an obituary, in effect (chapter 99), followed by the celebrated comparison between King Harald and his brother St Olaf in chapter 100:

King Harald, however, went to war for fame and power, and he forced everyone he could into submission; and so he was killed in another king's land.

Before that, however, Harald's career is told with a laconic detachment and lack of comment that conceals a cool irony. His personality is allowed to emerge in a series of episodes;

Snorri never tries to point the moral. For instance, when Empress Zoe in Constantinople accuses Harald of having misappropriated treasure which had been won in campaigns (chapter 13), nothing is said about whether these charges are true or not; the reader is left to recall for himself the casual comment about Harald in chapter 5, to the effect that:

All the booty he did not require for expenses he used to send by his own reliable messengers to Novgorod into the safe keeping of King Jaroslav. In this way Harald amassed a vast hoard of wealth....

One can see how effectively Snorri Sturluson dramatized history by comparing with contemporary Greek sources his whole treatment of Harald's Mediterranean adventures as a Varangian mercenary. Each of the episodes which Snorri relates (chapters 3–15) were designed to reveal aspects of Harald's character – his resourcefulness, his ambition, his cunning, his ruthlessness, his gift for leadership, his single-mindedness, his capacity for double-dealing. Whether the stories are true or not, they certainly create a vivid portrait.

By contrast, the Greek chronicler contents himself with a bare summary of Harald's activities:

Araltes [Harald] was the son of the king of Varangia [Scandinavia]; his brother was Julavos [Olaf], who inherited the kingdom at his father's death and made his brother, Araltes, his right-hand man in the kingdom. But while still a young man, Araltes decided to go on his travels and pay his respects to the blessed Emperor, Michael Paphlagon [Michael IV], and acquaint himself with Byzantine administration. He brought with him a company of 500 sturdy warriors. The emperor received him with all due honour and sent him with his company to Sicily, where the Byzantine army was campaigning [1038–41]. And Araltes went there and performed many great exploits. When Sicily had been conquered he returned with his company to the emperor, who appointed him *manglabites* [belt-wearer]. Then Delianos [Peter Delyan] started a rebellion in Bulgaria, and Araltes and his company went there with the emperor and performed great deeds against the enemy, as befitted a man of his courage and noble lineage [1041]. The emperor returned home after he had subjugated Bulgaria; and I, too, fought for the emperor to the best of my ability. And when we reached Mesina [?], the

Emperor appointed Araltes *spapharokandidates* [leader of the body-guard] in reward for his services. After the death of Emperor Michael [1041] and his nephew who succeeded him [Michael V, 1041–2], Araltes wanted permission from their successor, Constantine Monomachus, to return to his native country, but this he was forbidden to do, and difficulties were placed in his way. All the same, he managed to get away secretly, and became king in his own country. . . .

The outline and essence are broadly the same in the Greek chronicle and *King Harald's Saga*; but whereas the Greek chronicler is content with a recording of bare facts, Snorri's narrative of dramatic episodes is infinitely more effective as a means of portraying a man's personality.

Another technique Snorri employed as a story-teller, a saga-historian, was the use of recurrent themes. One of the episodes from the Varangian section is echoed later in the saga; it concerned Harald's almost obsessive concern with status and precedence. In chapter 4, he disputes with his superior, the Byzantine commander-in-chief Georgios Maniakes, the right to pick the best camping-site – and wins the dispute by a very cunning and underhand trick. Later, he tests the resolution of his nephew and co-king, Magnus the Good, under rather similar circumstances – over precedence at the royal jetty (chapter 27). This time, however, Harald has to give way in the face of Magnus's determination; and the double episode gives the reader an illuminating insight into the difference between the two kinsmen, Magnus the Good and Harald the Ruthless.

Throughout the saga, Snorri uses personality clashes of this kind as a means of illustrating character. King Harald's reign in Norway is, in effect, a series of these conflicts of personality. King Harald comes into conflict with Einar Paunch-Shaker, the independent-minded northern leader who stays loyal to the memory of King Magnus the Good and dares to stand up for the rights of his farmers – and is treacherously killed by Harald (chapter 44). Earl Hakon Ivarsson is popular with the king until his outstanding successes at the Battle of the Nissa stirs the king to jealousy; and when the king hears that Earl Hakon has chivalrously saved the life of King Svein Ulfsson of Denmark after the battle, King Harald is hell-bent on destroying this rival to his own popularity, at whatever cost (chapter 72).

The way that King Harald treats the Arnason brothers, Kalf and Finn, also demonstrates his way of wielding power. He is quite prepared to use Finn Arnason as a tool to smooth over a dangerous situation in the north after the murder of Einar Paunch-Shaker – and then cynically and contemptuously discards him, and arranges the death of his brother (chapter 52).

Another of these revealing personality clashes is described in chapters 36 and 37, when Snorri, in his detached way, describes the two Icelanders who fought for Harald all the way through the Varangian campaigns and returned to Norway with him. There was Ulf Ospaksson – loyal, unquestioning Ulf, who always did Harald's bidding without demur and was promoted to Marshal ('He was extremely shrewd and well-spoken, very capable, loyal, and honest') and who on his death received Harald's ultimate accolade ('There lies the most loyal and trusty liegeman a lord ever had'). Then there was Halldor Snorrason, a very different man indeed – dour, phlegmatic, imperturbable, according to Snorri, but who once, under stress, dared to accuse the king of timidity in battle (chapter 9) and was much too outspoken for the king's liking:

Halldor was a man of few words; he was blunt and outspoken, sullen and obstinate. The king found these traits disagreeable, as he had plenty of other men around him who were both well-born and eager to serve him.

Halldor preferred to go back to Iceland: he had seen enough of Harald the Ruthless – and Harald, as Snorri so subtly implied, was not the kind of king who appreciated home-truths.

In so many of these conflicts of personality, particularly in the long war with King Svein Ulfsson of Denmark, what emerges (but is never stated) is the moral superiority of the men whom Harald treats so unscrupulously and often treacherously. And yet a justification is also implied: that power has to be exercised firmly in order to safeguard authority. Snorri's readers could be expected to remember that Harald's brother, St Olaf, had been destroyed by a rebellion within his own kingdom, so Harald has to deal promptly and savagely with incipient opposition.

We suggested earlier in this Introduction that Snorri Sturluson's attitudes to kingship and power and politics had been considerably conditioned by his experiences of them, and his own life had taught him a curiously ambivalent, almost contradictory, attitude to kings. He had a deep respect for kingship – not necessarily for the individual king, but for the crown itself – and at the same time he feared it. A comparison with Snorri's text-sources shows that he always tended to minimize, or omit altogether, episodes that might bring the crown into disrepute. He minimizes the rivalry between King Magnus and King Harald as much as he can, and ignores the suggestion that Harald had actually made an uprising against his nephew. He omits altogether a smutty exchange between Harald and Empress Zoe in Constantinople.

Snorri is quite prepared to allow events to reveal King Harald as being mean, deceitful, vindictive, and intolerant; but he is not prepared to allow the throne to be insulted, if he can help it. Thus when, in chapter 66, he relates Earl Finn Arnason's insulting reference to the king's mistress ('No wonder you fought so lustily, if the mare was with you'), he goes out of his way to indicate why it was necessary to include something so distasteful and disrespectful to the throne:

It was then that Earl Finn uttered the insult that has long been remembered as showing how angry he was, since he could not curb his tongue.

Having lived at court as an honoured guest, having been appointed gentleman-in-waiting to King Hakon Hakonsson, it is not perhaps surprising that Snorri should feel this profound respect for kingship. But he had every reason to fear it, too. So much of his political life had been spent under the threat of interference from Norway; in 1220, when Snorri was in Norway, there had been plans to send a punitive naval expedition against Iceland, and Snorri himself had been instrumental in averting this. All the time that Snorri himself was striving to achieve power and wealth in Iceland against other chieftains, the Norwegian throne was casting a shadow over the land that grew steadily darker, and the struggle turned more and more into a choice between primitive democratic principles and authoritarian monarchy. Snorri seems to have tried to resist this interference from Norway, but there seems little doubt also that he was tempted to try to manipulate it to his own ends; he was to learn by terrible experience the ruthlessness of power when it was exercized by ambitious kings.

It was no doubt this close acquaintance with the Norwegian monarchy that gave Snorri his very distinctive attitude to national politics. He saw politics primarily as a matter of personal relationships – rather like a modern journalist – and it is this that makes the best saga-histories so vividly readable. Every action is motivated in terms of emotions – of loves and hates, of insults and humiliation, of ambition and vengefulness.

To Snorri, indeed, politics was a dirty business. No doubt it was the savagery and cruelty of the power struggles in thirteenth-century Iceland, in which he himself took such a prominent and sometimes dishonourable part, that coloured his political judgement and his attitude to King Harald; for Snorri's own lust for wealth and power was every bit as fierce and single-minded as King Harald's had been.

In this respect, it is a justifiable charge to suggest that Snorri's attitude to politics was too subjective for a historian – subjective to the point of being *simpliste*, even naïve. He did not see history in terms of political evolution, in terms of national movements, but only in terms of individual kings. He does not attempt to explore, for instance, the state of Norway as a nation in the aftermath of the civil war that brought St Olaf to his death. And when he writes of the long conflict between Norway and Denmark during King Harald's reign, it is not in terms of economic problems but only the rivalry between the two kings, culminating in the challenge to naval combat at the Battle of the Nissa.

And yet, near the end of the saga, Snorri reveals a flash of profound political insight in a conversation he presumably invented himself. Earl Tostig is in Norway, trying to persuade King Harald to invade England; and Tostig talks about success:

King Magnus won all Denmark because the chieftains there all supported him [he tells King Harald]; but you failed to win it because all the people there were against you. And King Magnus did not try to conquer England because all the people there wanted Edward as their king ... (chapter 79).

This explains, as nothing else could, why King Svein Ulfsson of Denmark, the man who lost every battle he fought, never lost his kingdom to King Harald; and it is a remarkably modern observation to come from a medieval historian.

When Snorri comes to deal with the events of 1066 he shows this same blend of acumen and over-simplification. With his intense concentration on the personal motivation of events, he clearly simplifies the question of why William of Normandy invaded England: it was, in Snorri's view, because Harold of England had insulted him by breaking off a betrothal to his daughter (chapter 95). The Norman chroniclers, who were committed to William's cause, saw it very differently. To them this was a holy war, a war of retribution against an oath-breaker – for Harold, they claimed, had sworn sacred oaths of allegiance to William; and William fought at Hastings with the blessing of the Pope and with consecrated relics round his neck.

Yet were they any more correct, in a real sense, than Snorri Sturluson? Snorri at least was uncommitted: Iceland was not involved at all in this triangle of ambition that erupted in England in the autumn of 1066. And Snorri seems to have had an almost instinctive understanding of the nature and character of the three men – a judgement with which today's historians are more and more inclined to agree.

Of William of Normandy, Snorri wrote: 'He was very shrewd, but said not to be trustworthy' (chapter 95).

Of Harald of Norway, Snorri wrote: 'He was brutal to his enemies and dealt ruthlessly with any opposition to him.'

But of Harold of England, Snorri told a very revealing story that showed him as a man of chivalry and honour. When the two kings, Norway and England, meet unwittingly before the Battle of Stamford Bridge, King Harald Sigurdsson's instinctive reaction was to regret a lost opportunity for treachery

– whereas Harold of England was generous in his praise of his formidable opponent.

Nearly two centuries after that fateful battle in Yorkshire, an Icelander in his library at faraway Reykholt wrote his account of what had happened. The details had become confused; the momentous battle he described was very different from the conflict that appears in his marvellously vivid pages. And yet, one feels, the men who took part in that year of destiny ring absolutely true; in *King Harald's Saga* Snorri Sturluson has given us a superb portrait of a remarkable king – a living, unforgettable portrait of the man who could well have changed the whole course of English history.

Scotland, 1966

MAGNUS MAGNUSSON
HERMANN PÁLSSON

Note on the Translation

HEIMSKRINGLA survives in several medieval manuscripts, some of which are fragmentary. It is generally agreed that the best text is to be found in the so-called *Kringla* vellum MS. which was written in Iceland *c.* 1260 and destroyed in the Great Fire of Copenhagen in 1728. However, two paper copies of this MS. had been made late in the seventeenth century, and it is on these that the standard edition of *Heimskringla* is based – in Íslenzk Fornrit, vols. 26–8, Reykjavik, 1941–51 edited by Bjarni Aðalbjarnarson. It is on that edition that this present translation of *King Harald's Saga* is based. The chapter headings are our own.

This is the first occasion that *King Harald's Saga* has been published in English as a separate saga, to the best of our knowledge; but *Heimskringla* as a whole has been translated into English several times previously : 'History of the Norse Kings', by the Orcadian Dr Samuel Laing, was published in three volumes in London in 1844, and reissued in the Everyman's Library series (Nos. 717, 722, 847). These have recently been reissued : *Part I, The Olaf Sagas* (Nos. 717, 722) has a new Introduction by Jacqueline Simpson, and *Part II, Sagas of the Norse Kings* (No. 847) has an Introduction by Peter Foote. *Heimskringla*, in four volumes, was included in their *Saga Library* by William Morris and Eiríkr Magnússon (Vols. 3–6, London, 1893). In 1932, Erling Monsen published a one-volume translation with the help of A. H. Smith (Heffer & Sons, Cambridge). The latest complete translation of *Heimskringla* is by Lee M. Hollander (University of Texas Press, 1964).

Our translation has been made independently of all these previous renderings.

One of the features of *King Harald's Saga* is the number of stanzas of Court Poetry embedded in the text. It has been our policy not to attempt a literal or a metrical version, but to try to convey in prose the salient information they contain; we have, however, tried to retain the basic rhythm and line-structure of the original, but made no attempt to reproduce the alliteration or internal assonance, or the highly esoteric metaphor.

Our treatment of proper names has been the same as in our previous translations of *Njal's Saga* and *The Vinland Sagas* (Penguin Classics, L103 and L154). As in these earlier volumes, we have relegated the genealogies to the footnotes, where they are printed in italics to differentiate them from our own comments.

We were tempted to include in this volume selected passages about King Harald's invasion of England from other medieval Icelandic sources, particularly *Morkinskinna*. Snorri Sturluson used *Morkinskinna* himself as one of his own sources for *Heimskringla* and omitted many pertinent passages from it – presumably because he could not accept their historical authenticity. On reflection, we decided to follow Snorri's example, and confine ourselves to the *Heimskringla* text.

This translation is dedicated to Professor Sigurður Nordal, doyen of Icelandic scholars, whose eightieth birthday (14 September 1966) coincides with the ninth centenary of King Harald's attempted conquest of England. In his lifetime, Dr Nordal has revolutionized the study of Iceland's saga literature; in particular he has done more than anyone else to illuminate the problems of *Heimskringla* and the literary achievements of Snorri Sturluson. We are much indebted to him, particularly for his book *Snorri Sturluson* (Reykjavik, 1920), and respectfully we offer him this translation as a token of our gratitude and appreciation.

We also owe a debt of gratitude to Mr A. J. A. Malkiewicz, M.A., of the Department of History at Edinburgh University, for his scholarly guidance on the historical background to the events described in this saga.

Finally, we would like to thank Mr William Hook, B.SC., who made a careful scrutiny of the text of the translation as usual, and contributed a great number of valuable improvements.

M.M.

H.P.

KING HARALD'S SAGA

1. The fugitive

HARALD SIGURDSSON was a half-brother of King Olaf the Saint; they had the same mother.[1] Harald took part in the Battle of Stiklestad where King Olaf was killed.[2] Harald was wounded in that battle, but managed to escape, along with many other fugitives. In the words of the poet Thjodolf Arnorsson:[3]

> *I heard that the storm of arrows*
> *Raged around King Olaf,*
> *And the king's young brother*
> *Fought beside him bravely.*

1. *Harald was the son of Sigurd Sow.*
Sigurd Sow (Halfdanarson) was one of the petty kings in tenth-century Norway; he ruled over Ringerike. Harald Sigurdsson's mother was Queen Asta Gudbrand's-daughter; her first husband, before Sigurd Sow, was King Harald of Westfold, and their son was Olaf Haraldsson (St Olaf).

2. King Olaf Haraldsson (St Olaf)) was King of Norway from 1016 to 1030, when he was killed at the Battle of Stiklestad, near Trondheim. Norway was still semi-pagan when Olaf Haraldsson came to the throne, and during his reign he fought ruthlessly against heathen practices. Eventually, the chieftains and farmers rebelled against him; King Olaf was driven from Norway, but later returned with a ragtag army. At Stiklestad he fought his last battle against overwhelming odds during an eclipse of the sun (31 August 1030), and died a martyr to the Christian faith. Miracles were reported within a few hours of his death, and he quickly came to be regarded as a saint; his cult spread through Scandinavia and western Europe, and also to Iceland and the British Isles, where several churches were dedicated to him (one of them, in London, is mentioned in chapter 57). The great Nidaros Cathedral in Trondheim, which is still being reconstructed, is dedicated to him. His life story is told in Snorri Sturluson's *St Olaf's Saga*.

3. Thjodolf Arnorsson was one of the many Icelanders who became Court Poets to the Norwegian kings. Several of his poems are still

Reluctantly, Prince Harald
Left King Olaf fallen
And went to secret hiding;
He was fifteen years old then.

It was Rognvald Brusason [1] who brought him from the battlefield and smuggled him to a remote farmhouse in a forest. There Harald's wounds were tended until he was fully recovered. After that the farmer's son escorted him east across the Kjolen Mountains; they kept clear of the main routes, using forest paths as much as they could. The farmer's son had no idea who his companion was; and as they were riding across from one wild forest to another, Harald composed this stanza:

Now I go creeping from forest
To forest with little honour;
Who knows, my name may yet become
Renowned far and wide in the end.

Harald travelled east across Jamtland and Halsingland, and from there into Sweden. There he met Earl Rognvald Brusason and many more of King Olaf's men who had escaped from the battle.

2. In Russia

NEXT spring they got some ships, and that summer they sailed east to Russia to the court of King Jaroslav and stayed with him over the winter.[2]

---

extant and are to be found scattered throughout many of the Kings' Sagas; but he is best known for his long eulogies in honour of King Magnus the Good (1035–47) and King Harald Sigurdsson.

1. Rognvald Brusason, who died *c*. 1046, was for several years Earl of Orkney. The history of the Norse Earls of Orkney is told in *Orkneyinga Saga*.

2. Jaroslav, the son of St Vladimir and great-great-grandson of Rurik, the founder of the Russian state, was sole ruler of Russia from 1036 to 1054; before that he had shared the kingdom with his brother Mstislav since 1019. He married Ingigerd, the daughter of

In the words of the poet Bolverk Arnorsson.[1]

> *You wiped blood from your greedy*
> *Sword when battle was over.*
> *You fed the ravens with corpses*
> *While wolves howled in the mountains.*
> *The next year, king of warriors,*
> *You spent east in Russia;*
> *Nowhere have I ever heard*
> *Of a greater soldier than you.*

King Jaroslav gave Harald and Earl Rognvald and their men a good welcome. He made Harald and Earl Rognvald Ulfsson's son, Eilif, commanders of his defence forces. In the words of the poet Thjodolf:

> *Side by side*
> *The two leaders fought;*
> *Shoulder to shoulder*
> *Their men lined up.*
> *They drove the Slavs*
> *Into defeat*
> *And gave the Poles*
> *Scant mercy.*[2]

Harald stayed in Russia for several years and travelled widely throughout the East. Then with a large following he set off on an expedition to Greece, and eventually he reached Constantinople. In the words of the poet Bolverk:

> *Bleak showers lashed dark prows*
> *Hard along the coast-line;*

King Olaf Eiriksson of Sweden (St Olaf addressed a series of love-poems to her before she became Queen of Russia). Jaroslav became the father-in-law of King Harald Sigurdsson of Norway (see chapter 17), King Andrew I of Hungary, and King Henry I of France.

1. Bolverk Arnorsson was the brother of Thojdolf Arnorsson. He, too, was one of King Harald's Court Poets.

2. Harald and Eilif must have taken part in the campaign waged by King Jaroslav against the Poles in 1031.

Iron-shielded vessels
Flaunted colourful rigging.
The great prince saw ahead
The copper roofs of Byzantium;
His swan-breasted ships swept
Towards the tall-towered city.

3. In Constantinople

AT that time, Empress Zoe the Great and Michael Catalactus were joint rulers of the Byzantine Empire.[1] As soon as Harald reached Constantinople he presented himself to the Empress and immediately joined her army as a mercenary; that very autumn he joined one of the galleys patrolling the seas east of Greece. Harald kept his own men together as a separate company. The commander-in-chief of the whole army was a man called Georgios,[2] a kinsman of the empress.

Soon after Harald joined the army, all the Varangians[3] became very attached to him, and they fought side by side in battle. Eventually Harald became the acknowledged leader of all the Varangians.

Georgios and Harald sailed to many of the Greek islands and inflicted heavy damage on the corsairs there.

1. Empress Zoe was first married (in 1028) to Emperor Romanos Argyros, but later she had him strangled in his bath. Zoe then married Michael IV, and they ruled from 1034 to 1041, when Michael died.

2. Georgios Maniakes; he led the Byzantine forces in campaigns in the Euphrates (1033–5) and Sicily (1038–40). There is no evidence to suggest that he really was kinsman to the empress.

3. The Varangians (*Væringjar*) were the Scandinavian warriors, mostly from Sweden, who served in the bodyguard of the Byzantine emperors. Byzantine sources do not mention them before 1034, but it is thought that they were operating in the days of Emperor Basil II (976–1025). After the Norman Conquest of England, large numbers of English soldiers joined the Varangian Guard, and in the

4. At odds with Georgios

ONCE on an overland march they had decided to camp for the night near a forest. The Varangians were the first to arrive in the area, and they chose the best place they could find for pitching their tents; it was on the highest ground, for the terrain was rather boggy and any rain would turn the lower ground into a swamp ill-suited for camping.

When Georgios, the army commander, arrived and saw where the Varangians had pitched their tents, he ordered them to move their camp elsewhere, saying that he wanted to pitch his own tents there himself.

But Harald said, 'If you arrived first at the night quarters, you would choose your own place and we would have to be content with pitching our tents elsewhere. In the same way, you can now camp anywhere you like – except here. I had assumed that it was the privilege of the Varangians here in the Byzantine Empire to be completely free and independent of all others, and to be beholden only to the emperor and empress to whom they owe their allegiance.'

They argued this fiercely, until finally they seized their weapons and were on the point of coming to blows. But wiser men intervened and separated them, and said it would be more sensible for them to settle the matter by clear agreement once and for all, to prevent similar disputes arising in the future. So a peace meeting was arranged by the best and wisest men, and there it was agreed with the consent of all parties that lots should be thrown on to a piece of cloth and that the Greeks and the Varangians should then draw the lots to decide which of them should take precedence when riding or rowing or putting in at harbour or choosing the ground for their tents. And the decision reached by the drawing of lots was to be binding on both sides.

---

latter years of the Byzantine Empire the Guard was composed almost entirely of Englishmen.

Now the lots were made. But before they were marked, Harald said to Georgios, 'I want to see how you are marking your lot, to make sure we do not mark our lots in the same way.'

Georgios agreed. Then Harald marked his own lot and threw it on to the cloth alongside the other. The man who had been chosen to draw the lots now picked one of them out and raised it aloft between his fingers and said, 'The owner of this lot shall take precedence when riding and rowing and putting in at harbour and choosing the ground for his tents.'

Harald seized his hand and snatched the lot away from him and hurled it into the sea. Then he said, 'That was my lot that was drawn.'

'Why did you not let everyone else see it?' demanded Georgios.

'Look at the one that's left,' said Harald, 'and you will recognize your mark on it.'

When the remaining lot was examined, everyone saw that it had Georgios's mark upon it; so it was decided that the Varangians should take precedence in all the matters that were in dispute.

Many other disagreements arose between them, and Harald always got the better of it in the end.

5. Among the Saracens

IN the summer all the forces went on a campaign together. Whenever the whole army was engaged, Harald saw to it that his own men were kept out of the battle or else were stationed where the danger was least; he claimed that he was anxious to avoid losses among his men. But whenever he and his men were engaged on their own, he drove them into battle so fiercely that they either had to be victorious or be killed. Thus it often came about that victories were won when Harald was in command, whereas Georgios did not succeed. The troops noticed this and said they would be better off if Harald were the sole commander of all the forces, and they criticized the general for his and his army's failures. Georgios retorted that the Varangians were refusing to support him, and told Harald to take his men away elsewhere and see what they could do by themselves, while he himself remained in command of the rest of the army. So Harald now left the main army, taking with him the Varangians and the Latin-speaking troops,[1] while Georgios remained in command of the Greek army.

It now quickly became apparent what each was capable of; for Harald gained victory and booty wherever he fought, whereas the Greeks went back to Constantinople – apart from some ambitious young warriors who were eager to share in the plunder, and who joined Harald's troops and accepted his command.

Harald now went with his army to Africa, to the parts which the Varangians call the Land of the Saracens.[2]

There he increased the strength of his army considerably, and captured eighty towns; some of them surrendered, and the others were taken by storm.

From there he went to Sicily. In the words of the poet Thjodolf:

> Bravely the young gold-giver
> Risked his life constantly,
> Capturing eighty cities
> In the Land of the Saracens;
> Then the young warrior,
> Scourge of the Saracens,
> Waged his grim game of war
> On the level plains of Sicily.

1. These 'Latin-speaking troops' were probably a band of Normans (who spoke French rather than Norse) who had been fighting under the Duke of Salerno before joining Georgios Maniakes on his campaigns in Sicily in 1038–40.

2. 'Africa' is probably a mistake here for Asia Minor. It is known that in the winter of 1034–5 the Varangians were heavily engaged in the western parts of Asia Minor, and in the following year there was constant fighting on the eastern borders of the Byzantine Empire, in the Caucasus.

In the words of Illugi the Brynjudale-Poet:[1]

> Harald, you forced the Mediterranean lands
> To submit to the great Emperor Michael
> (We have heard how Atli
> Invited his brothers-in-law home).[2] ...

This poem shows that Michael was the Greek Emperor at this time.

Harald spent several years in Africa and garnered there an immense hoard of money, gold and treasure of all kinds. All the booty he did not require for expenses he used to send by his own reliable messengers to Novgorod into the safe keeping of King Jaroslav.

In this way Harald amassed a vast hoard of wealth – not surprisingly, considering that he had been plundering in the richest parts of the world where gold and treasure are the most plentiful, and considering the scale of his achievements there: it has already been stated in all truth that he conquered eighty towns.

6. In Sicily

AS soon as Harald landed in Sicily he started plundering there too, and laid siege to a large and populous town. He surrounded it, because he realized that the walls were too stout

1. This Illugi, from Brynjudale in Iceland, was another of the Court Poets in Norway; very little is known about him.

2. The second couplet refers to a famous episode in Germanic heroic legend. King Atli (Attila) of the Huns determined to lay his hands on the famous Nibelung treasure, whose hiding-place was known only by his brothers-in-law, Hogni and Gunnar (Gundicarius of the Burgundians). He treacherously invited them home to a feast, and there tried to force them to reveal the secret. They both refused to tell him, and both died under torture, and the secret died with them.

It is not clear why the poet makes this allusion here, since most of the poem is lost. But it may have been intended to heighten the

to be broken down. But the townsmen had plenty of provisions and all other necessities to withstand a siege.

So now Harald thought up a scheme: he told his bird-catchers to catch the small birds that nested within the town and flew out to the woods each day in search of food. Harald had small shavings of fir tied to the backs of the birds, and then he smeared the shavings with wax and sulphur and set fire to them. As soon as the birds were released they all flew straight home to their young in their nests in the town; the nests were under the eaves of the roofs, which were thatched with reeds or straw. The thatched roofs caught fire from the birds, and although each bird could only carry a tiny flame, it quickly became a great fire; a host of birds set roofs alight all over the town. One house after another caught fire, and soon the whole town was ablaze.

At that all the people came out of the town, begging for mercy – the very same people who had been shouting defiant insults at the Greek army and its leader for days on end. Harald spared the lives of all those who begged for quarter, and took control of the town.

7. A stratagem

THERE was another town which Harald besieged with his army. This town, too, was populous, and so strongly fortified that there was no hope of taking it by storm. The town stood in the middle of an arid, level plain.

Harald told his men to dig a tunnel from a place where a stream flowed through a deep ravine that could not be seen from the town. They put the displaced soil into the water and let the stream carry it away. They toiled at this in relays day

---

dramatic colouring of the poem, by comparing Harald's perils to those of Gunnar and Hogni; or it may be an oblique reference to a later incident (chapter 14) when Harald tortured 'the Emperor Constantine X by blinding him.

and night. Meanwhile, the rest of the troops used to march up to the town every day, and the townsmen would take up position on the battlements and exchange shots with the attackers. At night, however, both armies rested.

When Harald reckoned that the tunnel was so long that it must now extend right inside the walls, he told his troops to arm themselves. They entered the tunnel just before daybreak; when they reached the far end, they dug upwards until they struck flagstones laid in lime. This was the floor of a stone-built hall. They broke through the floor and swarmed up into the hall. Inside, many of the townsmen were sitting eating and drinking, and were taken completely by surprise. The Varangians set on them at once with swords drawn, killing some of them while others managed to escape. The Varangians pursued them, while others captured the town gates and opened them. Now the main body of the army poured into the town, and at that the townsmen were routed; many begged for mercy, which was granted to all who surrendered.

That was how Harald captured this town, and with it a vast hoard of booty.

8. The third town in Sicily

THE third town they came upon was the largest and strongest of them all, and also the wealthiest and most populous. It was encircled by huge moats, and Harald realized that it could not be overcome by the same stratagems as the previous towns had been. They besieged the town for a long time without making any headway against it. At this, the townsmen were so emboldened that they drew up their troops on the walls, opened up the gates, and shouted at the Varangians, jeering at them and challenging them to come inside, telling them that they could fight no better than hens.

Harald told his men to ignore what the defenders were saying. 'We can achieve nothing by making an assault on the town,' he said. 'They can attack us with weapons from above, and even if we succeed in getting a party into the town they could easily shut our men inside if they want, and keep the rest of us outside, for they are in complete control of the gates. We shall therefore retaliate by showing them the same contempt, and let them see that we are not in the least afraid of them. Our troops are to go out on to the plain, as close to the town as possible, but taking care not to come within range of their weapons. They are all to be unarmed, and must indulge in sports, to show the townsmen that their troops do not cause us the slightest concern.

They kept this up for several days.

9. Halldor and Ulf

THERE were two Icelanders in Harald's company; one of them was Halldor Snorrason,[1] who brought this story to Iceland, and the other was Ulf Ospaksson.[2] They were men of exceptional strength and outstanding warriors, and were very dear to Harald's heart. They were both in the group taking part in the sports.

When all this had been going on for several days the townsmen became even bolder and started manning the walls un-

1. *Halldor was the son of Snorri the Priest.*

Snorri the Priest (d. 1031) was one of the leading chieftains in Iceland in the last decade of the tenth century and the first third of the eleventh century. He figures prominently in many of the sagas, including *Njal's Saga*, *Laxdæla Saga*, *Eyrbyggja Saga*, and *Grettir's Saga*.

His son, Halldor Snorrason, spent many years abroad, and there is an excellent account of his adventures in *Halldor's Story*.

One of Halldor's descendants was Snorri Sturluson, the author of this saga.

2. *Ulf was the son of Ospak, the son of Osvif the Wise.*

Ulf was a nephew of Gudrun Osvif's-daughter, the heroine of *Laxdæla Saga*. His great-grandson, Archbishop Eystein Erlendsson (see chapter 37, note 2), was one of the most influential men in twelfth-century Norway; he was archbishop from 1161 to 1188.

armed and leaving the gates open at the same time. When the Varangians observed this, they went to their sports one day hiding swords under their tunics and wearing helmets under their hats. When they had played at their games for a while they saw that the townsmen still suspected nothing; and suddenly they drew their weapons and made a rush at the gates. When the townsmen saw them coming they formed up fully armed and advanced to meet them. Battle was joined at the gates. The Varangians had no shields, so they wrapped their cloaks around their left arms; many were wounded and several killed, and soon they were all very hard pressed.

Harald was on the way from camp with the rest of his army to back them up; by then the townsmen were up on the battlements raining stones and missiles on the attackers, and a fierce battle was raging.

The Varangians who were fighting at the gates thought that relief was coming rather more slowly than they would have liked. As Harald came up to the gates his standard-bearer was killed. Harald then said to Halldor Snorrason, 'Halldor, you carry the standard.'

Halldor picked up the standard and said rather stupidly, 'Who would want to carry the banner before you, if you follow it as timidly as you have done today?'

But these words were spoken more in anger than in truth, for Harald was the bravest of warriors. Now they fought their way into the town. It was a fierce battle, but eventually Harald got the upper hand and captured the town.

Halldor Snorrason was severely wounded in the fight. He got a deep gash in the face, which left an ugly scar for the rest of his life.

10. The fourth town

THE fourth town Harald came to with his army was even bigger than all those which have been described already. It was so strongly fortified that there was no hope of taking it by storm. They laid siege to this town and blockaded it so that no supplies could reach it.

But when they had been there only a short while, Harald fell ill and took to his bed. He had his tent moved away from the main camp, for he found it more restful to be apart from all the clamour and clatter of the troops. As his men were constantly coming in groups to consult him, the townsmen realized that something was afoot in the Varangian camp, and sent spies to find out what was happening. When the spies got back to the town they reported that the leader of the Varangians was ill, which explained why there had been no assault on the town.

After a while Harald's strength began to fail, and this caused great concern and despondency among his men; and all this was reported to the townsmen. Eventually his illness became so critical that rumours of his death spread throughout the army. The Varangians now went to parley with the townsmen, told them that their leader was dead, and asked the priests to grant him burial inside the town. Many of the townsmen present at this meeting were in charge of monasteries and other important establishments there, and each of them was eager to have this corpse for his own church, because they realized that precious offerings would accompany it. So all the clergy donned their robes and came out of the town in a splendid procession, bearing shrines and other holy relics. The Varangians, too, formed up in a magnificent cortège, carrying the coffin on high under a canopy of precious cloth and many banners.

When the Varangians reached the gates they set the coffin down right across the entry, jamming open the gates. Then they sounded the call to arms on all their trumpets and drew their swords; the rest of the Varangian army came bursting out of the camp fully armed and rushed up to the town shouting their war-cries. The monks and other priests in the procession who had been competing to be the first to receive the offerings were now twice as anxious to be as far away as possible from the Varangians; for the Varangians killed anyone they could lay their hands on, priests and laymen alike: they rampaged through the whole town, killing all the inhabitants and plundering everything they could find.

They took an enormous amount of booty there.

11. Back to Constantinople

HARALD spent several years on these campaigns, both in the Land of the Saracens and in Sicily.[1] Then he went back to Constantinople with his troops and stayed there for a while before setting out on an expedition to the Holy Land.[2] He left behind all the gold he had been paid by the Byzantine Emperor, as did all the Varangians who went with him.

It is said that in all these campaigns Harald had fought eighteen battles. In the words of the poet Thjodolf:

> *All men know that Harald*
> *Fought eighteen savage battles;*
> *Wherever the warrior went*

1. In 1038, Emperor Michael sent an expedition under Georgios Maniakes to wrest Sicily from the Saracens. The Greeks captured practically the whole of Sicily, defeating the Saracens heavily at Messina and Tragina in 1040. Thereafter Georgios was removed from his command, but rebelled and tried to win the throne for himself – and was killed in battle in 1043. His successors in command threw away all the advantages Georgios had gained, and invaded southern Italy in an attempt to deal with the Normans there, but were severely defeated.

Other sources suggest that Harald Sigurdsson took part in both these campaigns, but that he left Italy early in 1041, and fought for the Byzantine Emperor against the Bulgarians later that year.

2. The Saga's chronology seems to have gone awry here. In 1036, Emperor Michael concluded a treaty with the Caliph of Egypt, which permitted the emperor to restore the damaged church that had been raised over Christ's grave. Harald seems to have been in command of the troops sent to escort the Byzantine craftsmen to Jerusalem. But this could scarcely have been after the Sicilian campaigns of 1038–41; it must have been soon after the treaty with the Caliph of Egypt was signed, in 1036 or 1037.

All hope of peace was shattered.
The grey eagle's talons
You reddened with blood, great king;
On all your expeditions
The hungry wolves were feasted.

12. To Jerusalem

HARALD went with his troops to the Holy Land and all the
way to Jerusalem; wherever he went in Palestine, all the towns
and castles were surrendered to him. This is how the poet Stuf
Thordarson,[1] who heard Harald's own account of these events,
described them :

> *With courage sharp as a sword-edge*
> *The all-triumphant warrior*
> *Left Greece to conquer Palestine –*
> *An easy task for Harald.*
> *With his overwhelming power*
> *The land fell to his army*
> *Unscorched and undisputed;*
> *May the Almighty protect him.*

The poet states there that Palestine submitted to Harald
without being laid waste by fire and sword. Harald then went
to the Jordan and bathed in the river, as is the custom of all
pilgrims. Harald gave treasure generously to the shrine at the
grave of Our Lord, the Holy Cross, and other sacred relics in
Palestine. He cleared a route all the way to the river Jordan,
killing all the robbers and other trouble-makers in the area. In
the words of the poet Stuf :

> *With shrewd and awful warnings*
> *The king imposed his justice*

1. Stuf Thordarson (Stuf the Blind) was the grandson of Gudrun
Osvif's-daughter, the heroine of *Laxdæla Saga*. There is an account
of his first meeting with King Harald Hardradi in *Stuf's Story*.

On both banks of the Jordan,
And curbed the robbers' power.
All the people could be certain
That swift punishment would follow
Any ill-deeds or transgression;
May his soul abide in Christ.

Then he went back to Constantinople.

13. Harald imprisoned

WHEN Harald returned to Constantinople from his expedition to Palestine, he was eager to visit Scandinavia and see his native land again; he had heard that his nephew, Magnus Olafsson, had become king of both Norway and Denmark.[1] So Harald now resigned his command with the Byzantine Emperor.

But when Empress Zoe heard about this she was furious, and brought charges against him: she accused him of having defrauded the emperor of treasure which had been won in campaigns under Harald's command.

Empress Zoe had a beautiful young niece called Maria; Harald had asked for her hand in marriage, but the empress had refused. Some Varangians who had been mercenaries in Constantinople brought north the story that according to well-informed people, Empress Zoe had wanted to marry Harald herself, and that this was her real complaint against Harald

1. Magnus Olafsson (King Magnus the Good) was an illegitimate son of St Olaf. For five years after St Olaf's death in 1030, Norway was ruled by a boy-king, Svein, the son of King Knut Sveinsson (Canute the Great). But such was his tyranny that Norway's chieftains sent a deputation to Russia, where Magnus Olafsson was staying at the court of King Jaroslav, to invite him to return to Norway as king. He was acclaimed king as soon as he reached Trondheim in 1035. He was elected King of Denmark as well in 1042 on the death of King Harda-Knut of Denmark.

His life-story is told in Snorri Sturluson's *Magnus the Good's Saga*.

when he wanted to leave Constantinople, although a different story was given to the public.

At that time the Byzantine Emperor was Constantine Monomachus,[1] who ruled the empire jointly with Empress Zoe. Because of these charges he now ordered Harald to be seized and taken to a dungeon.

14. Saved by a miracle

As Harald was approaching the prison, his dead brother, St Olaf, appeared to him in a vision and promised to help him (later, a chapel was built on that very spot in the street and dedicated to St Olaf; it is still standing).

The prison was a high roofless tower, with a door into the dungeon at street level. Harald was put in through this door, together with Halldor Snorrason and Ulf Ospaksson.

Next night a certain distinguished lady came to the prison with two servants. They scaled the wall with ladders, lowered a rope into the dungeon, and hauled up the prisoners. Saint Olaf had once healed this woman, and now he had appeared to her in a vision and directed her to rescue his brother Harald from prison.

Harald went at once to the Varangians, who all rose from their beds to greet him and welcomed him warmly. They all armed themselves and made their way to the chamber where the emperor lay sleeping. They seized the emperor, and put out both his eyes. This is how the poet Thorarin Skeggjason[2] described it in his poem:

1. Emperor Constantine Monomachus was Zoe's third husband, and ruled from 1042 to 1055. But once again, the saga's chronology seems to be at fault; the emperor at this time was Michael Calaphates, Michael V, 1041–2 (see next chapter).

2. Thorarin Skeggjason was the brother of another Court Poet, Markus Skeggjason, who was Law-Speaker of the Icelandic Althing from 1084 to 1107.

Harald won glowing gold,
But the Emperor of Byzantium,
Cruelly mutilated,
Lost the sight of his eyes.

In the words of the poet Thjodolf:

The warrior who fed the wolves
Ripped out both the eyes
Of the emperor of Byzantium;
Strife was unleashed again.
The warrior-king of Norway
Marked his cruel revenge
On the brave emperor of the East;
The Greek king had betrayed him.

In these two eulogies in honour of Harald, as well as in many other poems about him, it is stated that Harald himself blinded the Byzantine emperor. The poets would surely have attributed this act to a duke or count or some other man of rank if they had known that to be true; but this was the account brought back by Harald himself and the men who were with him.[1]

1. It was Emperor Michael Calaphates (1041–2) who was blinded, not his successor Constantine Monomachus (1042–55). The saga here undoubtedly echoes the cataclysmic events that took place in Constantinople in the spring of 1042. Michael Calaphates was the nephew of Michael IV, and became joint ruler with Empress Zoe at his uncle's death. In April 1042, he seized Empress Zoe, deposed her, and sent her to a convent. But the people of Constantinople rose against him and attacked the palace; the Varangian Guard, faithful to the empress, deserted the emperor. After fierce fighting, the emperor escaped to a monastery wearing monk's clothing. But the Varangians tracked him down there, and he was blinded in public. Empress Zoe now married Contantine Monomachus, who became emperor in his blinded predecessor's stead.

It may well be that the Varangians who blinded the emperor were led by Harald Sigurdsson, and that he had been released from prison during the popular uprising.

15. Harald's escape

THAT same night Harald broke into the apartments where the empress's niece, Maria, was sleeping, and carried her away by force. Then they went down to the Varangian galleys and took two of them. They rowed to the Bosporus, where they came to the iron chains which were stretched across the Sound. Harald told some of the oarsmen to pull as hard as they could, while those who were not rowing were to run to the stern of the galleys laden with all their gear. With that, the galleys ran up on to the chains. As soon as their momentum was spent and they stuck on top of the chains, Harald told all the men to run forward into the bows. Harald's own galley tilted forward under the impact and slid down off the chains; but the other ship stuck fast on the chains and broke its back. Many of her crew were lost, but some were rescued from the sea.

Thus Harald escaped from Constantinople and sailed on into the Black Sea. But before he put out to sea, he set Maria ashore with a good retinue to escort her back to Constantinople. He told her to tell her aunt, Zoe, how little power the empress had over him, for with all her might she could not have prevented him from marrying the girl.

Harald now sailed north to the Hellespont and from there past the eastern kingdoms. During this voyage he composed sixteen light verses, all ending in the same way. This is one of them:

> Round Sicily we sailed our ship
> With pride in all our hearts,
> Running like a forest stag
> Under a warrior crew.
> It's not for any land-lubbers
> To try that voyage again;
> Yet the golden lady in Russia
> Still spurns my suit.

The last couplet alludes to Elizabeth, the daughter of King Jaroslav of Novgorod.

16. Treasure

WHEN Harald arrived in Novgorod, King Jaroslav gave him a most cordial welcome. Harald stayed with him over the winter and took into his own keeping all the gold he had previously sent there from Constantinople, valuable treasure of all kinds. This hoard of wealth was so immense that no one in northern Europe had ever seen the like of it in one man's possession before. During his stay in Constantinople, Harald had three times taken part in a palace-plunder: it is the custom there that every time an emperor dies, the Varangians are allowed palace-plunder – they are entitled to ransack all the palaces where the emperor's treasures are kept and to take freely whatever each can lay his hands on.

17. Marriage

THAT winter, King Jaroslav gave his daughter Elizabeth in marriage to Harald; the Norwegians call her Ellisif. This is what the poet Stuf the Blind said about the marriage:

> The warlike king of Norway
> Won the match of his desire;
> He gained a king's daughter
> And a hoard of gold as well.

In the spring, Harald set off from Novgorod and travelled to the town at Lake Ladoga; there he got some ships and sailed off west in the summer. He first made for Sweden, and landed at Sigtuna. In the words of the poet Valgard of Voll:[1]

---

1. Very little is known about this particular Court Poet, Valgard of Voll; but he seems to have come from Voll, in the south of Iceland, and may have been descended from Valgard the Grey, who played a significant role in *Njal's Saga*.

Harald, you launched your vessel
Laden with a cargo of riches
Freighted with hard-won honour
And gleaming gold from Russia.
Through storm and gale, great king,
You sailed your plunging vessel;
And as the sea-spray was thinning
You sighted at last Sigtuna.

18. Svein Ulfsson

IN Sweden, Harald met Svein Ulfsson, who had been routed by King Magnus the Good at the battle of Helganess that autumn.[1] Harald and Svein greeted one another warmly; they were related by marriage.[2]

Harald and Svein joined forces and swore pledges of friend-

1. Svein Ulfsson was the son of Earl Ulf Thorgilsson, and nephew of King Knut Sveinsson (Earl Ulf was the husband of Knut's sister, Astrid, cf. chapter 78). Earl Ulf had been made regent over Denmark by Knut when Knut went to conquer England. When King Magnus the Good of Norway was elected King of Denmark in 1042, he installed Svein Ulfsson as Earl of Denmark, to rule as his regent. But Svein had claims on the throne himself, through his kinship with King Knut, and now he usurped the title of King of Denmark. Magnus the Good came over from Norway with an army to depose him and fought three battles with him, in each of which Svein was defeated. The third battle between them, at Helganess, on the east coast of Jutland, was fought in the autumn of 1045.

2. *King Olaf Eiriksson of Sweden was the maternal grandfather of Elizabeth, Harald's wife; and Svein Ulfsson's mother, Astrid, was King Olaf's sister.*

Harald's wife, Elizabeth, was the daughter of Ingigerd (King Olaf of Sweden's daughter), who married King Jaroslav of Russia (cf. note 2, page 46).

Svein Ulfsson's mother, Astrid, was half-sister to King Olaf of Sweden as well as being sister to King Knut of Denmark; Astrid and

ship. All the Swedes were Svein's friends, for he was related to the greatest family in the land. The Swedes now all became Harald's friends and supporters as well; Harald now had strong bonds of kinship with many important people. In the words of the poet Thjodolf:

> *The oak keel ploughed the ocean*
> *All the way west from Russia;*
> *And afterwards all the Swedes*
> *Gave you support, great king.*
> *Harald's gold-laden ship,*
> *Her sails stained with sea-spray,*
> *Listed hard to larboard,*
> *Scudding before the tempest.*

19. Campaign in Denmark

HARALD and Svein prepared a fleet and quickly gathered a large force. When the army was ready, they sailed west to Denmark. In the words of the poet Valgard of Voll:

> *The oak ship carried the eager*
> *Warrior prince from Sweden;*
> *Your proper inheritance*
> *Was still awaiting you.*
> *The square sail was straining*
> *At the mast rounding Skaane;*
> *On the flat Danish islands*
> *Maiden hearts were trembling.*

The fleet sailed first to Zealand, where they plundered and

King Olaf had the same mother, Queen Sigrid the Strong-Minded.
Thus, Harald and Svein Ulfsson were related by marriage through King Olaf of Sweden; Harald was Olaf's grandson-in-law, and Svein was Olaf's nephew.

burned extensively. From there they went on to Fyn Island and landed there and raided. In the words of the poet Valgard of Voll :

> Harald, you harried all Zealand
> And crushed all your opponents;
> The wolves came running swiftly
> To rend the battle-fallen.
> On Fyn your mighty forces
> Stormed across the island;
> Helmets there were tested,
> Ornate shields were shattered.
>
> Bright flame burned in a village
> Not far south of Roskilde;
> Tirelessly, King Harald,
> Your fires devoured the buildings.
> Many Danes lay fallen,
> Death cut off their freedom;
> In silent grief the others
> Crept to hide in forests.
>
> Stumbling, the survivors
> Scattered from the carnage,
> Sorrowing they fled to safety,
> Leaving their women captured.
> Maidens were dragged in shackles
> To your triumphant longships;
> Women wept as bright chains
> Cruelly bit their soft flesh.

20. King Magnus

IN the autumn after the battle of Helganess, King Magnus the Good had sailed north to Norway. Then he heard that his uncle, Harald Sigurdsson, had arrived in Sweden and made an alliance with Svein Ulfsson, and also that they had set off with a large force and were planning to conquer Denmark and then Norway. King Magnus levied troops throughout Norway, and soon gathered a huge army. Then he heard that Harald and Svein had reached Denmark and were burning and looting everything they found, and that the Danes were submitting to them all over the land.

It was also said that Harald was much taller and stronger than most men, and so shrewd that nothing was impossible for him, for he always won the victory wherever he fought; and that Harald was also so wealthy that no one knew his equal. In the words of the poet Thjodolf:

> Now the seafaring warriors
> Have little hope of peace;
> Fear stirs in men's hearts,
> Warships lie off the beaches.
> Death-dealing King Magnus
> Will sail his vessels southwards,
> While Harald's ocean-dragons
> Are pointing to the north.

21. Peace moves

KING MAGNUS the Good's counsellors declared that in their opinion it would be a tragedy if Harald and his nephew King Magnus were to bear arms against one another. Many of them offered to try to bring about a settlement between them, and the king was persuaded to agree to this. Messengers were sent off in a fast cutter to hurry south to Denmark, where reliable Danish friends of King Magnus undertook to make an approach to Harald. All this was arranged in the greatest secrecy.

When Harald was told that his nephew, King Magnus, was prepared to offer him a reconciliation and a half-share in the Norwegian kingdom, in return for an equal division of their combined wealth, he sent secret messages back to King Magnus.

22. Treachery

ONE evening a little later, when Harald and Svein were drinking and talking, Svein asked him which of his treasures he valued most highly. Harald replied that it was his banner, 'Land-Waster', that he treasured most. Svein asked what there was about the banner to make it so valuable. Harald replied that the banner was said to bring victory to the man before whom it was borne into battle – and that had been so ever since he got it.

'I will believe in the banner's magic power,' said Svein, 'only when you have fought three battles against your nephew King Magnus and won all three of them.'

Harald retorted angrily, 'I am well aware of my kinship with Magnus without needing you to remind me of it. And even though we are now at war with one another, there is no reason why he and I could not have a much more agreeable meeting.'

Svein flushed deep red and said, 'Some people say, Harald, that the only pledges you have honoured in the past are those you thought would profit yourself best.'

'You know of fewer occasions when I have violated my pledges,' replied Harald, 'than those on which King Magnus could claim that you have broken faith with him.'

And with that they parted, each to his own quarters.

Later in the evening when Harald was going to bed in the fo'c'sle of his ship, he said to his servant, 'I am not going to sleep in my own bed tonight, for I suspect there is treachery afoot. I noticed earlier this evening that my kinsman Svein greatly resented my plain speaking. Keep watch here tonight, to see if anything happens.'

Harald then put a log of wood in his usual bed, and went elsewhere to sleep.

During the night a boat was rowed over to the ship; a man came clambering aboard and ripped aside the tenting of the fo'c'sle. He went inside and struck at Harald's bed with a huge axe, sinking it deep into the log that lay there. Then he jumped down into his boat again and rowed away into the dark night, leaving the axe embedded in the log as evidence.

Harald now woke his men and told them about this treachery.

'It is all too obvious,' he said, 'that we do not have the strength here to cope with Svein if he is going to use treachery against us. Our best hope is to slip away from here while we still can, so let us now cast off our ships and row away stealthily.'

They did so, and rowed away through the night north along the coast; they travelled day and night without pause until they came to where King Magnus was lying with his army. Harald went before his nephew, King Magnus, and there was a joyful reunion. In the words of the poet Thjodolf:

> You split the ocean with your keels,
> Far-travelled king of men,
> When sailing west from Denmark;
> Fine ships ploughed the flood-tide.
> King Magnus offered to share
> Half his lands and men with you;
> When royal kinsmen met,
> The reunion was a joyful one.

After that the kinsmen talked, and their discussions were most conciliatory.

23. Sharing the crown

KING MAGNUS was lying at anchor close to the shore, and had a camp on land. He invited his uncle Harald to join him at his table, and Harald came with sixty men. It was a splendid feast.

Late in the day, King Magnus went to the tent where Harald was sitting. With the king came several men bearing bundles of weapons and clothing. The king went up to the man sitting nearest to the door and gave him a good sword; to the next he gave a shield, and to all the others he gave clothing, weapons, or gold, the more costly the more important the receiver.

Finally he came to his uncle Harald, and now he was holding in his hand two reed-straws.

'Which of these straws will you accept?' he asked.

'The one next to me,' replied Harald.

Then King Magnus said, 'With this reed-straw I give you half of Norway, together with all its dues and duties and all the estates within it. And I also declare that you shall be king as lawfully as I over every part of Norway. But whenever we are together, I am to be accorded precedence in greetings, in attendance, and in rank; and when there are three royal personages together, I shall sit in the middle. In harbour, I shall have the royal berth and the royal jetty. And in return for giving you a rank and position which I had never intended to grant anyone for as long as I lived, you are to support and strengthen our kingdom.'

Harald now rose to his feet and thanked him handsomely for the honour and high title he had conferred on him. After that they sat down together, and spent the rest of the day in the highest spirits.

In the evening, Harald and his men returned to their ships.

24. Sharing the wealth

NEXT morning King Magnus sounded the trumpet to assemble the whole army; and when the assembly was convened, he announced publicly the gift he had made to his uncle Harald. And at this assembly, Thorir of Steig conferred the title of King on Harald.[1]

That same day King Harald invited King Magnus to his table; Magnus came with sixty men to Harald's camp ashore, where

1. Thorir of Steig and Harald were cousins; Thorir was the nephew of Asta, the mother of both St Olaf and Harald.

a feast had been prepared. At this feast the two kings sat side by side on the same high-seat. It was a splendidly lavish banquet, and both kings were happy and cheerful.

Later in the day King Harald had a large number of chests brought into the tent; his men also carried in bundles of clothing, weapons, and other valuables, all of which he distributed among those of King Magnus's men who were present at the feast.

Then he had the chests opened, and said to King Magnus: 'Yesterday you gave me a great kingdom which you had wrested from your enemies and mine, and you made a partnership with me. That was generously done, for you had fought hard for it. For my own part, I have spent much time in foreign lands and had to undergo not a few hazards in order to amass this gold you now see before you. Now I want to share this wealth with you. We shall own all this money equally, just as we share the kingdom of Norway jointly between us. I know that our temperaments are not the same, for you are much more generous than I; so we shall divide this money into two equal parts, and each of us can do with his own share whatever he wants.'

Harald then had a huge ox-hide spread out on the floor, and the gold was emptied on to it out of the chests. Then scales and weights were produced, and the whole treasure was divided into two equal parts. All those present were astonished that such immense wealth in gold should have been assembled in Scandinavia in one place. All this wealth, however, rightly belonged to the Byzantine emperor, who is said to own whole houses crammed with red gold.

The kings were now very merry. Then a large ingot of gold as big as a man's head came up. King Harald picked it up and said, 'Where is the gold, nephew, that you can match against this lump?'

King Magnus replied, 'All the wars and huge levies have so reduced my resources that all the gold and silver I have left is what I have on my person. I now have no more gold in my possession than this one bracelet.' And with that he took off the bracelet and gave it to Harald.

Harald looked at it and said, 'This is a very small piece of gold, nephew, for a king who owns two kingdoms. And yet there are some who would doubt your claim even to this bracelet.'

King Magnus replied gravely, 'If I am not the rightful owner of that bracelet, then I do not know what I can rightly call my own, because my father, the sainted King Olaf, gave me that bracelet when we parted for the last time.'

King Harald replied, laughing, 'That's quite true, King Magnus: your father gave you this bracelet – after he had taken it from my father for some trifling reason. It's also true that it was not an easy time for minor kings in Norway when your father was at the height of his power.'

At this feast King Harald gave Thorir of Steig a bowl carved from maple wood; it was hooped with gilded silver and had a silver handle, also gilded. The bowl was filled with new-minted silver coins. There were also two gold bracelets, which together weighed one mark. The king also gave Thorir his own cloak of brown purple lined with white fur, and promised him high honours and his friendship. Thorgils Snorrason[1] once saw the altar-cloth which was later fashioned from this cloak, and he has stated that Thorir's granddaughter, Gudrid, told him that she herself had seen the maple-bowl when it was in the possession of her father, Guthorm Steig-Thorisson.

In the words of the poet Bolverk Arnorsson:

> The green land of Norway
> Came into your power,
> Open-handed Harald,
> When you gave gold to Magnus.
> The pact between you kinsmen
> Was kept in peaceful concord,
> But strife was now awaiting
> The usurper Svein of Denmark.

1. Thorgils Snorrason (d. 1201) was the son of Snorri Hunbogason the Law-Speaker (d. 1170). Thorgils was a clergyman who lived at Skard, in the west of Iceland.

25. Joint rule

KING MAGNUS and King Harald ruled Norway jointly for a
year following their reconciliation, but each kept his separate
court. During the winter they went on circuit through the
Uplands, sometimes together and sometimes separately. They
travelled all the way north to Trondheim and the Trondelag.

Since his return to Norway, King Magnus had looked after
the holy remains of St Olaf; every year he had the hair and
nails trimmed, and he himself kept the key of the shrine. Many
miracles took place at the holy shrine of St Olaf.

It was not long before differences arose between the two
kings, and many people were wicked enough to try to provoke
discord between them.

26. Svein Ulfsson

SVEIN ULFSSON had been asleep when Harald had stolen
away, but afterwards he made inquiries about where he had
gone. When Svein heard that Harald and Magnus had made a
treaty and joined forces, he sailed with his army to the east
coast of Skaane and stayed there until he heard in the winter
that Magnus and Harald had moved north to Norway with
their forces. Then Svein returned with his army to Denmark,
and appropriated all the royal revenues that winter.

27. Kings at variance

IN the spring, King Magnus and King Harald raised levies from
Norway. One night it happened that both kings lay in the same
harbour, and next morning King Harald was ready to sail before
King Magnus, and put out to sea first. That evening he arrived

first at the harbour where he and King Magnus were planning to spend the night; Harald now moored his ships at the royal berth and put up the deck-awnings.

King Magnus had set sail somewhat later, and by the time he reached the harbour Harald's men had finished putting up the awnings. Magnus and his men could see that Harald had moored his ships at the royal berth and intended to remain there. So when they had lowered their sails, King Magnus said to his men, 'Man all the oars on both sides and get ready to row, while the rest of you get your weapons out and arm yourselves. If Harald and his men will not move off, then we shall fight.'

When King Harald realized that King Magnus was prepared to fight it out with them, he said to his men, 'Cut the moorings and get the ships out of this berth! Nephew Magnus is angry!'

They did so, and moved the ships away from the berth, and King Magnus moored his own ships there.

Later, when both sides had settled in, King Harald went with several men on board King Magnus's ship. The king greeted him cordially and welcomed him aboard.

King Harald said, 'I had thought we were come among friends, but a short while ago I began to doubt whether you wanted it to be so. However, it's a true saying that "youth is always hasty"; I shall regard your conduct as no more than a mark of youth.'

King Magnus replied, 'It was a mark of my birth, not my youth, that I should remember what I have given and what I have withheld. If this trivial matter had been allowed to go by default, there would soon have been another. I want to honour our agreement in every respect, and I expect you to observe my rights in the same way.'

'It is also an old custom that it is the wiser man who must always give way,' said King Harald. And with that he went back to his ship.

Such exchanges between the kings showed clearly how delicate the situation was. King Magnus's men maintained that he was in the right, and the more foolish of them claimed that Harald had been rather slighted. But King Harald's men said that the agreement had only been that King Magnus should have precedence when the two kings reached harbour together, and that Harald was not obliged to move out of the berth if he had arrived there first; they maintained that Harald had acted sensibly and with great restraint. But those who wanted to make trouble out of it argued that King Magnus was wanting to disown the agreement and had done Harald an injustice and had insulted him.

Disputes of this kind gave rise to so much foolish talk that it led to further disagreements between the kings themselves. There were many other signs to show that they did not see eye to eye, although very little of that is recorded here.

28. King Magnus dies

KING MAGNUS and King Harald sailed with their army south to Denmark; and when Svein Ulfsson learned of their coming, he fled east to Skaane. The kings spent most of the summer in Denmark and subjugated the whole country. They spent the autumn in Jutland.

One night when King Magnus was asleep in his bed, he dreamed that he was with his father King Olaf the Saint; and in the dream St Olaf said to him, 'Which would you prefer, my son: to come with me now, or to live to be the most powerful of kings and grow very old – but also to commit such a crime as you would scarcely ever, if at all, be able to expiate?'

In his dream, Magnus answered, 'I want you to choose for me.'

Then he dreamed that St Olaf said, 'You are to come with me.'

King Magnus told his men this dream; and a little later he fell ill and lay on his sick-bed at a place called Suderup. As death neared he sent his half-brother Thorir with a message to Svein Ulfsson, asking him to give Thorir any help he needed; and with this message, King Magnus bequeathed the Danish kingdom to Svein, saying that it was proper that Harald should rule over Norway and Svein over Denmark.

After that, King Magnus the Good died, and was deeply mourned by everyone.[1] In the words of Odd the Kikina-Poet:[2]

> *Tears were shed when the good*
> *King was carried to his bier:*
> *A sad and heavy burden*
> *For those whom he had given gold.*
> *Grief-stricken, his courtiers*
> *Could scarce keep back their tears;*
> *And sorrowing, his people*
> *Have mourned him ever since.*

29. King Harald

AFTER this, King Harald assembled all his forces and announced that he intended going to the Viborg Assembly with the army to have himself declared King of Denmark; then he was going to subjugate the whole country. He regarded Denmark as his lawful inheritance from his nephew King Magnus, no less than Norway. He asked the army to give him full support, and declared that the Norwegians would then be the rulers of the Danes for ever.

It was Einar Paunch-Shaker [3] who answered the king; he said he felt it a more urgent duty to bring his friend, King Magnus, to his final resting-place beside St Olaf than to fight wars abroad or to covet another king's lands or possessions. He concluded by saying that he thought it better to follow King Magnus dead than any other king alive. Then Einar had the king's body

1. King Magnus died on 25 October 1047.
2. Little is known about this Court Poet, and only a handful of his verses have survived.
3. Einar Paunch-Shaker was one of the most powerful men in the north of Norway. He had opposed King Olaf the Saint during his reign, but after St Olaf's death, it was Einar who instigated the uprising that brought St Olaf's son, Magnus the Good, to the throne of Norway in 1035. Einar remained Magnus's staunchest supporter and counsellor.

dressed in magnificent robes and laid out where it could be seen from King Harald's ship.

All the Trondelag men and most of the other Norwegians now made ready to sail back home with King Magnus's body, and the expedition against Denmark broke up. King Harald realized that it would be best for him to go back to Norway and secure that kingdom first, and then raise reinforcements from there. So King Harald sailed back to Norway with the whole army; and as soon as he reached Norway he held assemblies there and had himself proclaimed king in all parts of the country; he travelled west from Oslo Fjord, and was accepted as king in every province of Norway.

30. The funeral

EINAR PAUNCH-SHAKER and all the forces from Trondelag escorted Magnus's body and took it to Trondheim; it was buried at St Clement's Church, where St Olaf's shrine then rested.

King Magnus had been of average height, with regular features and a fair complexion and fair hair. He was well-spoken and quick-thinking; he was noble-minded and exceptionally generous with his wealth, a great warrior and very courageous in battle. He was the most popular of kings, and was praised by friend and foe alike.

31. Svein's vow

SVEIN ULFSSON had been staying at Skaane that autumn, and was setting out on a journey east to Sweden; he was planning to renounce the royal title which he had assumed in Denmark. But as he was about to mount his horse, some men came riding up to him and told him the news that King Magnus the Good was dead, and that the whole Norwegian army had gone from Denmark.

Svein replied at once: 'I swear before God that I will never flee from Denmark again as long as I live.'

He mounted his horse and rode south through Skaane, and quickly gathered a large force there. That winter he subjugated the whole of Denmark, and the Danes all accepted him as their king.

King Magnus's half-brother, Thorir, came to King Svein in the autumn with the late king's message, which was described earlier. King Svein gave him a good welcome, and Thorir remained with him for a long time in high favour.

32. Raiding

KING HARALD SIGURDSSON assumed the crown over the whole of Norway after King Magnus's death. The following spring, after he had ruled the country for one winter, he raised a levy throughout the entire kingdom, mobilizing half of his full army in men and ships. With this force he sailed south to Jutland and plundered and burned there extensively that summer. When he sailed into Randers Fjord, King Harald composed this stanza:

> Our vessels lie at anchor
> Here in Randersfjorden,
> While ladies in night-linen
> Croon songs to their husbands.

Then he called on the poet Thjodolf to complete the stanza. Thjodolf added:

> Next year our cold-blooded anchor
> Will drop in warmer oceans;
> Thus I read the future:
> We shall cast our anchor deeper.

In his poem, the poet Bolverk confirms that Harald went south to Denmark the summer after King Magnus's death:

Next year you raised a levy
In the fair land of Norway;
Waves caressed the gunwales
As your fleet ploughed the ocean.
A host of splendid vessels
Lay on the blue billows,
Laden with hardy warriors;
The Danes watched in terror.

They burned down the farm of a great chieftain called Thorkel Geysa, and carried off his daughters in chains to the ships because they had made derisory remarks the previous winter about King Harald's plan to invade Denmark; they had carved anchors out of cheese, and said that these could easily hold all the king of Norway's ships. This was what was composed about it:

The mocking Danish maidens
Carved useless anchors
Out of their crumbling cheeses;
Norway's king was angry.
Today these very maidens
Can see the iron anchors
Holding his eager warships;
And none is laughing now.

It is reported that the watchman who first caught sight of King Harald's fleet said to Thorkel Geysa's daughters, 'I thought you said that Harald would never come to Denmark.'

'That was yesterday,' replied Dotta.

Thorkel Geysa paid a huge ransom for his daughters. In the words of the poet Grani:[1]

Relentlessly the warrior
Wreaked his vengeance on them;
The Danish girls of Hornwood
Had no chance to dry their tears.

1. Very little is known about this Icelandic Court Poet, and only a few fragments of his work have survived.

The wrathful king of Norway
Drove his foes to his longships;
Dotta's chieftain father
Had to pay huge ransom.

King Harald plundered Denmark all that summer and amassed an immense hoard of wealth there. But he did not establish himself there that summer, and in the autumn he went back to Norway and spent the winter there.

33. Marriage again

THE winter after King Magnus's death, King Harald married Thora, the daughter of Thorberg Arnason. They had two sons; the elder was called Magnus, and the younger Olaf. King Harald and Queen Elizabeth had two daughters; one was called Maria, and the other Ingigerd.[1]

In the spring following the expedition that has just been described, King Harald raised another levy and went back to Denmark to plunder; and he kept this up every summer. In the words of the poet Stuf:

Falster was laid waste, I hear.
The people cried with terror,
The ravens fed on corpses;
Each year the Danes trembled.

1. There is no evidence that Thora ever became Queen of Norway; Queen Elizabeth was still alive at this time (cf. chapter 82). She seems to have been King Harald's concubine, after the fashion of the Byzantine emperors. But her sons, Magnus and Olaf, jointly succeeded to the throne of Norway after King Harald's death (cf. chapter 101).

Thora's father, Thorberg Arnason, was the brother of Finn and Kalf Arnason, who play an important part later in this saga (chapter 45 ff.).

34. Svein and Harald

KING SVEIN ruled over the entire Danish kingdom after the death of King Magnus the Good. He spent the winters in quiet, but in the summers he called up his army, threatening to go north to Norway with the Danish forces and wreak no less havoc there than King Harald was causing in Denmark.

One winter King Svein challenged King Harald to meet him at the Gota River the following summer and fight it out to a finish, or else make a treaty. For the rest of the winter both kings were busy preparing their ships, and the following summer they called up half their armies.

That summer Thorleik the Handsome[1] came from Iceland to compose a poem about King Svein Ulfsson. When he arrived in Norway he was told that King Harald had already sailed south to meet King Svein at the Gota River; this is what he then composed:

> *The battle-hardy farmers*
> *Of Trondelag will be meeting*
> *The warlike king of Denmark*
> *On the ship-strewn ocean.*
> *God alone will decree now*
> *Which king will rob the other*
> *Of life and all his lands;*
> *Svein cares little for broken pledges.*

> *Often Harald of Norway*
> *Has launched his bristling vessels;*
> *Now he sails in anger*
> *South across the ocean;*
> *While King Svein's sea-dragons,*
> *Gold-mouthed, brightly-painted,*
> *A host of deadly warships,*
> *Are straining to sail northward.*

1. Nothing more is known about this poet.

King Harald arrived at the meeting place with all his forces, and heard there that King Svein was lying with his fleet in the south, off Zealand. King Harald then divided his army; he sent most of the peasant levy back home, but kept his courtiers and his landed men, the cream of his fighting-men, and also all the farmers who lived nearest to the Danish border.[1] With this force he went over to Jutland, south of Skagen, and then made his way south through Thy province, putting everything to the sword. In the words of the poet Stuf:

> In haste the men of Thyland
> Fled before King Harald;
> Harald's lust for battle
> Brooked no opposition.

They went all the way south to Hedeby, and captured the town and burned it. One of King Harald's men composed this:

> All Hedeby was blazing,
> Fired by Harald's fury;
> There's no limit to the courage
> Of Norway's warrior sea-king.
> Svein now feels the havoc
> Of Harald's deadly vengeance.
> At dawn in Hedeby's outskirts
> I saw the tall fires raging.

Thorleik the Handsome also refers to this in his poem, after hearing that the proposed battle at Gota River had not taken place:

> Men who have heard nothing
> Ask the returning warriors
> Why the vengeful Harald
> Vented his rage on Hedeby,
> That time when Norway's sea-king
> Without cause brought his longships
> West to King Svein's township,
> One year of evil memory.

1. At that time the Danish kingdom extended into what is now southern Sweden; the Gota River marked the boundary between Norway and Denmark.

35. Encounter

AFTER this, Harald went back north with sixty ships; most of them were large and heavily laden with the booty they had taken that summer. As they sailed north past Thy province, King Svein came down to the coast with a huge army and challenged King Harald to come ashore and fight. King Harald's army was less than half the size of Svein's army; so he challenged Svein to a sea-battle instead. In the words of the poet Thorleik the Handsome:

> Svein was born the luckiest
> King in all the world;
> He challenged Norway's army
> To blood their shields ashore.
> Heedless of flight, Harald
> Preferred to fight on shipboard,
> When the warrior king of Denmark
> Held the land with his army.

After that, Harald sailed north to Skagen; but then the wind turned against them and they lay to in the shelter of the island of Læso for one night. Then a thick sea-fog came down. When the sun rose next morning, they saw what seemed to be a host of fires burning on the other side of the sea. King Harald was told of this; and when he saw it he said at once, 'Pull down the awnings and take to your oars! The Danish army is upon us! The fog must have lifted where they are, and the sun is shining on their gilded dragon-prows.'

It was just as he said: King Svein of Denmark was there with a huge force. Both fleets now rowed as hard as they could. The Danish ships were faster under oars, and the Norwegian ships were water-logged and heavily laden, so the distance between them steadily narrowed.

Harald, whose own dragon-prowed ship was bringing up the rear, realized that this would not do. He ordered his men to throw some planks overboard and lay out clothing and other valuables on them. The sea was so calm that the planks drifted with the current; and when the Danes saw their own possessions floating past on the sea, the leading ships turned in that direction, for they thought it easier to pick up what was floating about than to seek it on board the Norwegian ships. So the pursuit slowed down.

But when King Svein came up he urged his men on fiercely, saying that it would be a great disgrace for such a huge army if they could not overtake and capture an enemy with such a small force. The Danes now began to row hard again; and when King Harald saw that the Danish ships were coming faster, he ordered his men to lighten their ships as much as possible and throw overboard the malt, flour and bacon, and also to break open the wine-casks. This helped for a while. Then Harald ordered the bulwarks and empty casks and barrels to be thrown overboard, and also the Danish prisoners they had taken that summer. When King Svein saw them floating about in the sea, he gave orders for them to be rescued; but so much time was lost doing this that the Norwegians got away. The Danes now turned back, and the Norwegians sailed on their way. In the words of the poet Thorleik the Handsome:

> I heard how Svein of Denmark
> Chased the Norwegian longships
> Across the sea; but Harald
> Escaped the Danish vengeance.
> Harald's hard-won plunder
> Was tossed into the waters
> Of the stormy Jutland sea;
> He also lost some vessels.

King Svein turned back with his fleet to the island of Læso, where he came upon seven Norwegian ships; they were part of the levied force, and were manned only by farmers. When King Svein came at them they begged for quarter and offered ransom for their lives. In the words of the poet Thorleik the Handsome:

> Harald's peasant seamen
> Begged King Svein for mercy;

Outnumbered, the Norwegians
Bought their lives with ransom.
The brave Norwegian farmers
Refused to fight a battle,
Preferred instead to parley;
They would not risk their lives.

36. Harald and the Icelanders

KING HARALD was a powerful king and ruled his kingdom firmly; he was so shrewd a man that it is generally agreed that there was never a king in Scandinavia to match him in profound wisdom and acumen. He was a great and fearless warrior, very strong and better skilled at arms than any other man, as has already been said. But many more of his feats and achievements have not been written about here, partly because of our lack of knowledge, and partly because we are reluctant to place on record stories that are unsubstantiated. Although we have been told various stories and have heard about other deeds, it seems to us better that our account should later be expanded than that it should have to be emended.

A great deal of information about King Harald is contained in the poems which Icelandic poets presented to him and his sons; and because of his interest in poetry, he was a great friend of theirs.

He was also, indeed, a great friend to all the Icelanders. Once when there was a severe famine in Iceland, King Harald permitted four ships to sail to Iceland with flour, and he decreed that the price should not exceed a hundred lengths of homespun for three hundredweights.[1] He also allowed all the poor who could get themselves a passage from Iceland, to come to Norway. And thus the country survived, until conditions improved. King Harald also sent out to Iceland a bell for the

---

1. This famine began in 1056.

church which had been built for the Althing at Thingvellir [1] with timber provided by St Olaf.

Such are the memories of King Harald that people in this country still cherish, as well as the many great acts of generosity that he showed to people who stayed with him.

Halldor Snorrason and Ulf Ospaksson, who were mentioned earlier, had come to Norway with King Harald. They were very different men in many ways. Halldor was a huge, exceptionally powerful man, and very handsome; of him, King Harald testified that Halldor was the most imperturbable man in the face of the unexpected that he had ever had. Whatever the circumstance, whether it was dire peril or joyful news or anything else, Halldor was neither more nor less cheerful, nor would he lose any sleep over it, nor eat nor drink any less or more than was his custom.

Halldor was a man of few words; he was blunt and outspoken, sullen and obstinate. The king found these traits disagreeable, as he had plenty of other men around him who were both well-born and eager to serve him.

Halldor stayed with the king for only a short while. He went back to Iceland and took up farming at Hjardarholt,[2] and lived there until old age.

1. The kernel of the Icelandic republic was the Althing (General Assembly), which was instituted in 930. It was held annually in the open air for two weeks late in June at Thingvellir ('Assembly Plains'), and was the main judicial, legislative, and social event of the year. Legislative and judicial authority was in the hands of the chieftains, who combined religious and secular power and had the title of goði. The Althing was an oligarchic institution, but the chieftains' power depended on the voluntary allegiance of their supporters, the freeholding farmers.

2. Hjardarholt, in Laxriverdale, was built by Olaf the Peacock in the late tenth century; his son was Kjartan Olafsson, one of the principal characters in Laxdæla Saga.

37. Ulf Ospaksson

ULF OSPAKSSON stayed on with King Harald in great favour and affection. He was extremely shrewd and well-spoken, very capable, loyal, and honest. King Harald made Ulf his Marshal, and gave to him in marriage his own sister-in-law Jorunn.[1] Ulf and Jorunn had two children: Jon the Powerful of Rosvold,[2] and Brigida.[3]

King Harald made Marshal Ulf a landed man, and gave him estate-dues worth twelve marks, and a half-province in Trondelag as well, as Stein Herdisarson says in his poem about Ulf.[4]

38. Churches in Trondheim

KING MAGNUS THE GOOD had built St Olaf's Church at Trondheim over the spot where the saint's body had lain for a night; this was just behind the town as it was then. King Magnus had also founded a royal residence there.

The church had not been completed when King Magnus died, so King Harald had it finished. King Harald also made preparations for a stone hall to be built at the royal residence; but before it was completed he began to build St Mary's Church up on the sandhill close to the spot where the holy remains of St Olaf had been interred the first winter after his death. This was

1. *Jorunn was the daughter of Thorberg and sister of Thora, King Harald's wife* (cf. chapter 33).

2. *Jon the Powerful was the father of Erlend the Flabby, the father of Archbishop Eystein and his brothers.*

Rosvold is in Værdale, north of Trondheim.

3. *Brigida was the mother of Sheep-Ulf, the father of Burden-Peter, the father of Ulf the Tiny and the others.*

4. Stein Herdisarson's great-grandfather was the brother of Ulf's grandfather; Stein was also related to the poet Stuf the Blind. No trace of his poem about Ulf remains; it may well have been a funeral poem.

a large minster, and so strongly built with mortar that it was very difficult to break it down when Archbishop Eystein had it moved.[1]

St Olaf's holy relics were kept in St Olaf's Church while St Mary's Church was being built.

King Harald had a royal residence built on the bank of the river Nid, just below St Mary's Church, where it still stands to this day. The stone hall he had had built for the old residence he converted into a church, which he dedicated to St Gregory.

39. Hakon Ivarsson

THERE was a man called Ivar the White; he was a landed man and of noble lineage, and had estates in the Uplands. His mother was the daughter of Earl Hakon the Powerful.[2] Ivar was an exceptionally fine-looking man.

Ivar had a son called Hakon, who is said to have surpassed all his contemporaries in Norway for courage, strength, and accomplishments. In his youth he took part in raiding expeditions and earned a great name for himself. Hakon Ivarsson became a man of great distinction.

40. Einar Paunch-Shaker

EINAR PAUNCH-SHAKER was the most powerful of all the landed men in Trondelag at this time. He and King Harald were not on very good terms, but Einar retained all the estate-dues

1. In 1178, Archbishop Eystein moved St Mary's Church to El-gesæter in Trondheim, where it became the abbey church; this was to make room for the massive Nidaros Cathedral that stands in its place to this day.

2. Earl Hakon Sigurdsson the Powerful was one of the most prominent men in Norway in the second half of the tenth century. He seized the throne of Norway in 975, and ruled as king until he

he had had while King Magnus was alive. He was extremely wealthy.

Einar was married to Bergljot, the daughter of Earl Hakon the Powerful, who has been mentioned already. Their son, Eindridi, was fully grown by then; he was married to Sigrid Ketil's-daughter, King Harald's niece.[1] Eindridi took his appearance and fine looks from his mother's side of the family, from Earl Hakon the Powerful and his sons; but from his father Einar Paunch-Shaker he had inherited great strength and stature and all the accomplishments in which Einar was outstanding.

Eindridi was extremely well liked.

41. Earl Orm

THERE was an earl in the Uplands at that time who was called Orm; he was a grandson of Earl Hakon the Powerful.[2] He was a man of great distinction.

Earl Hakon's granddaughter Sigrid [3] was married to a man called Aslak Erlingsson, who lived at Sola, in Jæderen, at that time.

Another of Earl Hakon's granddaughters, Gunnhild, was married to King Svein Ulfsson of Denmark.

These were some of Earl Hakon's descendants in Norway at this time, and many other distinguished people besides; all his kin were much more handsome than other people and most of them were outstandingly capable, and all of them were people of distinction.

---

was killed (by a slave, in a pigsty) in 995; his successor on the throne was King Olaf Tryggvason (995–1000).

1. *Sigrid was the daughter of Ketil Kalf and of Gunnhild, King Harald's sister.*

2. *Earl Orm's mother was Ragnhild, the daughter of Earl Hakon the Powerful.*

3. *Sigrid was the daughter of Earl Svein, the son of Earl Hakon the Powerful.*

42. King Harald

KING HARALD was a very autocratic ruler, and his imperiousness increased as his position in Norway grew more secure. It came to the point that scarcely anyone dared to argue with him, or to propose anything which was different from what he himself wanted. In the words of the poet Thjodolf:

> *Subjects of King Harald*
> *Must show their subjection*
> *By standing up or sitting*
> *Just as the king wishes.*
> *All the people humbly*
> *Bow before this warrior;*
> *The king demands obedience*
> *To all his royal orders.*

43. Friction with Einar

EINAR PAUNCH-SHAKER was the chief leader of the farmers throughout Trondelag; he was their spokesman at assemblies when the king's agents were taking action against them. Einar was very skilled at law, and he did not lack the courage to plead his cases openly at these assemblies, even when the king himself was present. All the farmers supported him.

The king was enraged by this, and it came to the point that they exchanged angry words. Einar said that the farmers were not prepared to allow the king to violate the law in trying to deny them their legal rights. Disputes of this kind occurred several times between them.

Einar now began to keep a large following of men at home on his estates, and an even greater force whenever he came to Trondheim when the king was there.

On one occasion Einar went to the town with a large force –

eight or nine longships and almost five hundred men – and when he reached Trondheim he came marching in with all these men. King Harald was in his residence there, and from the balcony he watched Einar's force disembarking. It is said that Harald then composed these stanzas:

> *I see sailing through the town*
> *With a host of warlike followers*
> *Generously paunched Einar,*
> *Skilled plougher of the ocean.*
> *The stout chief is hoping*
> *To fill the throne of Norway;*
> *Even kings, I sometimes feel,*
> *Keep smaller courts than his.*
>
> *Einar of the flailing sword*
> *Will drive me from this country*
> *Unless I first persuade him*
> *To kiss my thin-lipped axe.*

Einar stayed in the town for several days.

44. Murder

ONE day a court was held, at which the king himself was present. A thief who had been caught in the town was brought before the court; this man had previously been in Einar's service, and Einar had taken a liking to him.

Einar was told of this and realized that the king would be even less likely to let the man off if he knew that Einar had an interest in the case. So Einar told his men to arm themselves and accompany him to the court; and there Einar took the accused man away by force.

After this, mutual friends took steps to bring about a reconciliation between Einar and the king; and eventually a peace-meeting was arranged where the two were to meet in person.

There was an audience-room at the royal residence down by

the river. The king went into it with several of his men, leaving the rest of his company in the courtyard outside. The king then had shutters placed over the skylight, so that there was only a small opening left.

When Einar came into the courtyard with his men he said to his son Eindridi, 'You stay outside with the rest of the men, and then there will be no danger to me.'

So Eindridi remained outside by the door.

Einar went inside and said, 'How dark the king's audience-room is!'

At that moment the king's men set on him, hacking and thrusting. When Eindridi heard the noise he drew his sword and rushed into the room, but he too was struck down at once, like his father. The rest of the king's men now ran over to the audience-room and lined up before the door; but the farmers, with no one to lead them, stood irresolute. Each urged the other on, saying that it was a great disgrace for them not to avenge their leader, but no attack came of it.

The king now came out and joined his men; he drew them up in battle array and raised his banner, but still the farmers failed to attack. Then the king boarded his ship with all his men, and they rowed away down the river and out into the fjord.

Einar's wife, Bergljot, was told of his killing; she was staying in the house they had taken in the town. She hurried to the king's residence at once, where the farmers were still waiting, and urged them to fight; but by then the king was already rowing away down the river.

Bergljot said, 'We could have done with my kinsman Hakon Ivarsson now! Eindridi's killers would not be rowing down the river now if Hakon had been here on the bank.'

After this, Bergljot had the bodies of Einar and Eindridi dressed, and they were buried in St Olaf's Church, near the tomb of King Magnus the Good.

After Einar's death King Harald was so hated for this murder that only the lack of a leader to raise the standard prevented the landed men and farmers from doing battle with the king.

45. Finn Arnason

AT that time one of King Harald's landed men, Finn Arnason,[1] was living at Austratt, in Orland; he was married to Bergljot Halfdan's-daughter, King Harald's niece,[2] and King Harald's wife, Thora, was Finn Arnason's niece.

Finn Arnason and his brothers were all very attached to the king.

Finn had spent several summers on Viking expeditions to the British Isles, and with him on these raids had been Hakon Ivarsson and Guthorm Gunnhildarson.[3]

King Harald now sailed down Trondheimsfjord and went to Austratt, where he was given a cordial welcome. He and Finn Arnason talked about the events that had just taken place, the killing of Einar and his son Eindridi, and the hatred and hostility which the Trondelag farmers had for the king.

Finn said sharply, 'What a hopeless scoundrel you are! You do one evil thing after another, and then you are so frightened that you don't know what to do with yourself!'

The king laughed and said, 'I am going to send you in to Trondheim now, kinsman; I want you to get the farmers to make peace with me. And if that fails, I want you to go to the Uplands and settle matters with Hakon Ivarsson so that he will not be against me.'

'How are you going to reward me if I go on this dangerous mission?' asked Finn. 'The men of Trondelag and the Uplands

1. Finn Arnason played a leading part in Norwegian politics in the first half of the eleventh century. He and his five brothers were alternately supporters and enemies of St Olaf, and helped to bring King Magnus to the throne. His brother, Thorberg Arnason, was the father of King Harald's wife, Thora (cf. chapter 33).

2. *Bergljot was the daughter of Halfdan, the son of Sigurd Sow; Halfdan was a brother of King Harald, and half-brother to St Olaf.*

3. Guthorm Gunnhildarson (cf. chapter 54) was the son of Ketil Kalf and of Gunnhild, King Harald's niece. His sister was Sigrid, the widow of Eindridi Einarsson (cf. chapter 40).

now hate you so bitterly that none of your emissaries would be safe to go there unless he had some influence with them.'

'Go on this mission, Finn,' said the king, 'for I know that you are the only man who could bring about a reconciliation between us; and you can ask me any favour you choose.'

Finn said, 'Keep your word, then, and I shall choose the favour I want: I want you to grant to my brother Kalf peace and safe residence here in this country again, and restore to him all the possessions and rank and authority he had before he left the country.'[1]

The king agreed to everything that Finn stipulated, and they shook hands on this in the presence of witnesses.

Then Finn said, 'What am I to offer Hakon Ivarsson to persuade him to accept a settlement? He is now the chief leader of these Trondelag men.'

'First you must find out what terms Hakon himself demands for a settlement,' said the king. 'Then you must argue on my behalf as well as you can; but ultimately you can promise him anything but the kingdom itself.'

After this, King Harald went south to More, where he gathered a large force.

46. The mission

FINN ARNASON went to Trondheim with his followers, nearly eighty strong; and when he reached the town he held a meeting with the townsmen. At this meeting, Finn made a long and eloquent speech, urging the townsmen and farmers above all not to let themselves be so swayed by hatred for their king as to drive him from the country; he reminded them of all the evils that had befallen them after they had done the very same

1. Finn's brother, Kalf Arnason, had been one of the leaders of the army that fought against St Olaf at Stiklestad, and Kalf may have dealt St Olaf his death-blow (Kalf's brothers, however, fought on St Olaf's side). Soon after King Magnus the Good came to the throne, Kalf Arnason fell out with him and fled the country.

thing to St Olaf. He also said that the king was willing to pay whatever compensation for these killings the best and wisest men might determine.

At the end of Finn's speech, the men agreed to let the matter rest until the messengers Bergljot had sent to Hakon Ivarsson in the Uplands returned.

Then Finn went with all his companions out to Orkdale and from there up to the Dovre Mountains and east across them. He went first to see his son-in-law Earl Orm (the earl was married to Finn's daughter, Sigrid), and told him about his mission.

47. The agreement

THEN they arranged a meeting with Hakon Ivarsson. When they met, Finn told Hakon why he had come and what King Harald was offering. It was soon clear from what Hakon said that he regarded it as a solemn duty to avenge his kinsman Eindridi; he added that he had received word from Trondelag that he would get plenty of support there for a rebellion against the king. But Finn explained to Hakon how much more it would be to his advantage to accept from the king the highest honours he himself could choose, rather than to risk starting a war against the very king to whom he owed allegiance – a war he was certain to lose, anyway: 'In which case you would have forfeited your life and property. But if you succeeded in bringing the king down, you would only be called a traitor.'

Earl Orm supported Finn's arguments; and when Hakon had thought it over he spoke his mind: 'I am prepared to make terms with King Harald on condition that he gives to me in marriage his kinswoman Ragnhild, King Magnus Olafsson's daughter, with such a dowry as befits her and is to her own liking.'

Finn said he would agree to that on the king's behalf, and they made a binding agreement on these terms. And with that, Finn went back north to Trondheim.

Now all the unrest and rebellion died down. The king retained his kingdom intact and there was peace in Norway, for now the alliance which Eindridi's kinsmen had formed against the king had been broken.

48. Hakon's wooing

WHEN the time came for Hakon Ivarsson to claim what had been promised to him in the secret agreement he went to see King Harald. They talked together, and the king said that he for his own part intended to honour fully the agreement that Finn had made.

'And now, Hakon,' said the king, 'you must go and discuss this matter with Ragnhild and see whether she is willing to consent to the marriage. No one, neither you nor anyone else, can hope to win Ragnhild for a wife without her full consent.'

So Hakon went to see Ragnhild and made her a proposal of marriage.

Ragnhild replied, 'How often am I made to feel that my father King Magnus is dead and gone! Particularly now, if I am expected to marry a mere farmer, however handsome or accomplished you may be. If my father King Magnus had been alive, he would not have married me to anyone less than a king; it is not to be expected now that I would want to marry a man without any title at all.'

Hakon now went back to King Harald and told him of his conversation with Ragnhild, and reminded him also of the agreement Finn had made with him; Finn himself was present on this occasion, and several of the men who had witnessed their agreement. Hakon cited them all as his witnesses that it had been agreed that King Harald was to provide Ragnhild with a dowry to her liking: 'Now that she refuses to marry an untitled man, you must confer a title upon me. I have lineage enough to deserve the title of earl, and many other qualities as well, according to most people.'

The king replied, 'My brother, King Olaf, and his son King Magnus, allowed only one earl at a time in the kingdom during their reigns, and I have done the same since I became king; I am not going to deprive Earl Orm of the title I have already given him.'

Hakon Ivarsson now realized that his hopes were not going to be fulfilled, and he was furious; Finn, too, was very angry. They accused the king of breaking his word, and with that they departed.

Hakon Ivarsson left the country immediately. He had a well-manned longship, and now he sailed south to Denmark, where he went at once to see his kinsman King Svein Ulfsson.[1] The king greeted him most cordially and gave him fine estates in his country. Hakon now took over command of the land-defences against the Vikings who often harried the coasts of Denmark – the Wends and other Slavs as well as the Letts.[2]

He lived on board his warships both winter and summer.

49. Asmund

THERE was a man called Asmund who is said to have been King Svein's nephew and foster-son. Asmund was an exceptionally fine-looking man, and the king loved him dearly. But as Asmund grew up, he became very unruly and took to killing. This displeased the king, and he sent Asmund away from the court, and gave him good estates which should have been enough to keep him and his company in comfort.

As soon as Asmund received this royal grant, however, he gathered around him a large force of men; but the revenues which the king had granted him did not suffice for all his ex-

1. King Svein was married to Earl Hakon's granddaughter, Gunnhild (cf. chapter 41), and Hakon Ivarsson was Earl Hakon's great-grandson (cf. chapter 39).

2. Wendland was the name given generally to cover the regions of the Baltic coast from Holstein eastwards.

travagance, so he seized for himself some much larger estates which belonged to the king. When the king heard of this he summoned Asmund to him; and when they met, the king ordered him to stay at court – without his own retinue. Asmund had no choice but to obey.

But after only a short time at the court with the king, Asmund could endure it no longer; one night he ran away and rejoined his men, and now he started causing even more trouble than before.

Later, when the king went on circuit through the kingdom, he passed near the place where Asmund was staying; so he sent a party of men to take him by force. The king had him put in irons, and kept him prisoner for some time, hoping that this would calm him down. But as soon as Asmund was released from his shackles he ran away again, and got some men and warships. He then began plundering both in Denmark and abroad, causing great havoc, killing and looting far and wide.

The people who suffered most from these outrages came to the king and complained to him about their losses.

The king said, 'Why are you telling me all this? Why don't you go to Hakon Ivarsson? He is in command of my land-defences, charged with preserving the peace for you farmers and punishing all Vikings. I had been told that Hakon was a man of bravery and courage, but now it seems to me that he shuns all the places where he thinks there might be any danger.'

These remarks by the king were told to Hakon Ivarsson, with many additions. Hakon then set off with his men in search of Asmund. They met at sea, and Hakon attacked at once. There was a long and fierce battle, and Hakon boarded Asmund's ship and cleared it. Eventually Hakon and Asmund came face to face and fought; Asmund was killed, and Hakon cut off his head.

Hakon now hurried back to see King Svein. The king was sitting at table; Hakon walked up to the table and laid Asmund's head in front of the king, and asked him if he recognized it. The king made no reply, but flushed deep red. Then Hakon went away.

A little later the king sent messengers to Hakon, ordering him to leave his service. 'Tell him', the king had said, 'that I have no wish to do him any harm; but I cannot answer for all my kinsmen.'

50. Hakon returns to Norway

HAKON now left Denmark and went back north to his estates in Norway. His kinsman, Earl Orm, was dead by then. Hakon's friends and kinsmen were all very pleased to see him, and a number of nobly born men undertook to bring about a reconciliation between him and King Harald. Eventually they came to terms: King Harald gave Hakon the earldom and authority which Earl Orm had had, and Hakon married Princess Ragnhild. In return, Hakon swore oaths of loyalty and service to King Harald, as was his duty.

51. Kalf returns to Norway

KALF ARNASON had been raiding in the British Isles since he left Norway; during the winters he usually stayed in Orkney with his kinsman Earl Thorfinn.[1]

Then Kalf's brother, Finn, sent word to him telling him of the private agreement he had made with King Harald, whereby Kalf was to be free to live in Norway and recover all the estates and revenues he had had under King Magnus the Good. When Kalf received this message he made ready to leave at once, and sailed east to Norway. First he went to see his brother

1. Earl Thorfinn Sigurdsson – Thorfinn the Mighty – was the greatest of the Norse earls of Orkney; he ruled for about fifty years, from 1014 to c. 1065. He was married to Ingibjorg, the daughter of Finn Arnason; so Kalf was his uncle-in-law.

Finn, and when Finn had arranged safe conduct for him, Kalf went to see the king himself in person, and they made their reconciliation on the terms that the king and Finn had previously agreed in private.

Kalf pledged himself to all the duties he had previously owed to King Magnus, binding himself to perform all the services which King Harald required of him for the good of his kingdom. Kalf then recovered all the estates and revenues he had had before.

52. Death in Denmark

NEXT summer King Harald raised a levy and went on an expedition south to Denmark, where he plundered until the autumn. But when he came south to Fyn Island there was a large army lying in wait for them there. The king ordered his men to disembark, and prepared to make a landing. Drawing up his order of battle, he put Kalf Arnason in charge of a company and ordered him to make the first landing, and told him where he was to head for; he said he himself would be following closely to give them support.

Kalf went ashore at once with his company and soon came face to face with the enemy force. Kalf went into the attack immediately, but the battle did not last long, for Kalf was soon overwhelmed and routed. The Danes pursued Kalf's company, and many of the Norwegians were killed, including Kalf himself.

King Harald now went ashore with the main force; soon after landing they came across the slain men on the battlefield, and quickly found Kalf's body. It was taken down to the ships, while the king pushed farther inland, plundering and killing many people. In the words of the poet Arnor Thordarson:[1]

1. Arnor Thordarson, nicknamed 'the Earls'-Poet', was for a long time Court Poet to the Norse earls of Orkney in the eleventh century. He presented to King Harald Sigurdsson a eulogy which is now lost.

The king dyed crimson
His sword on Fyn Island.
Islanders lost their lives there,
Flames devoured their houses.

53. Finn's decision

AFTER this, Finn Arnason was filled with hatred for the king because of the killing of his brother Kalf. Finn felt that the king himself had not only schemed Kalf's death, but had also deliberately deceived Finn into luring his brother Kalf back to Norway into the king's power and pledge. When all this became known, many people felt that Finn had been very gullible ever to have believed that Kalf would gain King Harald's trust, considering how vindictive the king could be over smaller offences than those which Kalf had committed against him.

The king let people say what they liked about it, and would neither confirm nor deny the accusation. But it was quite obvious that the king was very pleased about what had happened; this is the verse that King Harald himself composed about it:

Now I have caused the deaths
Of thirteen of my enemies;
I kill without compunction,
And remember all my killings.
Treason must be scotched
By fair means or foul
Before it overwhelms me;
Oak-trees grow from acorns.

Finn Arnason was so bitter over this whole affair that he left the country and went south to Denmark; he went to see King Svein, who gave him a good welcome. They talked for a long time in private, and eventually Finn became King Svein's liegeman; in return he was appointed Earl of Halland, and charged with defending it against Norwegian attacks.

54. Guthorm

THERE was a man called Guthorm Gunnhildarson,[1] who was a nephew of St Olaf and King Harald. From his earliest manhood, Guthorm was extremely accomplished. He often used to stay with King Harald, who valued him highly as a friend and a counsellor, for Guthorm was a shrewd man; he was also very popular.

Guthorm often went on Viking expeditions and plundered extensively in the British Isles with a large force. He enjoyed asylum and permission to winter at Dublin, in Ireland, and was on friendly terms with King Margad.[2]

55. Guthorm and Margad

THE following summer King Margad and Guthorm went on a joint expedition to plunder in Wales, and acquired there an immense amount of booty. Afterwards they sailed into the Menai Strait to divide the spoils. When King Margad saw the great hoard of silver that was produced he claimed it all for himself, ignoring entirely his friendship with Guthorm. It enraged Guthorm that he and his men should be deprived of their share; but the king told him there were only two courses open to him: 'One is to accept my decision with good grace, and the other is to fight – the winner to take all. And in addition, you are to leave your ships, for I want them for myself.'

Guthorm thought the choice very difficult. It seemed to him a great humiliation to have to surrender his ships and his share of the booty without just cause; but it was also highly danger-

1. *Guthorm was the son of Ketil Kalf and Gunnhild of Ringnes.*
2. King Margad (Eachmargach in Irish), the son of Rognvald Ivarsson, was king in Dublin from 1035 to 1038 and from 1046 to 1052. He was of mixed Norse and Irish descent.

ous to fight the king and the huge army he had with him – the odds were overwhelming, for the king had sixteen longships, and Guthorm only had five. So Guthorm asked the king to give him three days' grace so that he could discuss the matter with his men, hoping that during that time he might be able to soften the king's attitude and with the help of his men's entreaties, make him more friendly. But the king refused his request.

This was on the eve of St Olaf's Day.[1]

Guthorm now decided that he would die with honour or win the victory, rather than submit to humiliation and disgrace and derision at having lost so much. He called upon God and his kinsman St Olaf, asking them for help and support, and vowed to give to St Olaf's Church one tenth of all the booty they would get if they won the victory.

Then he drew up his force in battle array against this vast army and charged into the attack. And with the help of God and St Olaf, Guthorm won the victory. King Margad was killed, and with him every single one of his followers, both young and old.

After this sublime victory, Guthorm went back home joyfully with all the spoils they had gained by this battle. And every tenth coin of all the silver they had won they took to St Olaf as promised – a vast amount of money. From this silver, Guthorm had a crucifix fashioned in an image which is either of himself or his fo'c'sleman; the statue stands ten feet tall. This crucifix Guthorm gave to St Olaf's Church, where it has stood ever since as a memorial to Guthorm's victory and to St Olaf's miracle.

56. A Danish duke

THERE was an evil and envious duke in Denmark who had a Norwegian concubine from Trondelag. This woman worshipped St Olaf and believed steadfastly in his sanctity, but the duke disbelieved everything he was told about the miracles of

1. 28 July 1052.

this holy man; he said it was nothing but hearsay and gossip, and ridiculed all the praise and worship which the people gave to this good king.

When the feast-day of St Olaf approached, the day on which this gracious king lost his life and which all Norwegians kept holy, the foolish duke refused to observe it; and on the day itself he ordered his concubine to bake a loaf of bread in the oven.

The woman knew the duke's temper all too well, and knew that he would punish her cruelly if she failed to carry out his command. So, much against her will, she set to work and heated the oven. She wept and wailed as she worked, and called upon St Olaf, saying that she would never believe in him again if he did not avenge this outrage in some way or other.

And now you shall hear of a most fitting punishment and a true miracle: for at one and the same moment, the duke became blind in both eyes, and the woman's bread turned to stone!

Fragments of that stone are now in St Olaf's Church and many other places.

St Olaf's Day has been regularly observed in Denmark ever since.

57. Miracle in London

IN France, there was a sick man who was so crippled that he could only crawl on his hands and knees. One day when he was out on the roadway he fell asleep. He dreamed that a noble-looking man came to him and asked where he was going; and the cripple named a certain village.

But the noble-looking man said to him, 'Go to St Olaf's Church in London, and then you shall be cured.'

The cripple woke up and set off at once for St Olaf's Church. Eventually he reached London Bridge, and there he asked the townspeople if they could tell him where St Olaf's Church was; but they all replied that there were so many churches in London that they could not possibly know to whom each of them was dedicated.

A little later, however, a stranger came up to him and asked him where he was going. The cripple told him, and the man then said, 'Let us go to St Olaf's Church together, then, for I know the way.'

They made their way across the bridge and along the street which led to St Olaf's Church. When they came to the lich-gate the stranger stepped across the threshold of the gate; but the cripple rolled himself over it, and stood up at once, completely cured. When he looked about him, his companion had vanished.[1]

58. Stratagem in Denmark

KING HARALD founded the town of Oslo and was often in residence there, for it was easy to get supplies there from the extensive cultivated land all around. It was also well placed for defending the country against the Danes, and as a base for raids on Denmark. King Harald often went raiding in Denmark, although he never took a very large force with him.

One summer King Harald put to sea with a small number of light skiffs and a small force of men. He sailed south down Oslo Fjord, and when the wind was favourable he sailed across to Jutland and began raiding; but the inhabitants gathered forces and defended their country.

So King Harald sailed on and went into Limfjord. This fjord has a very narrow channel at its mouth, but farther inside it seems as wide as the open sea. Harald made raids on both sides of the fjord, but wherever he went the Danes had forces ready to meet him.

King Harald then brought his ships to a small uninhabited

---

1. This St Olaf's Church was in Southwark. There were other churches in England dedicated to St Olaf, in York and Exeter, for instance.

island to get water. But when they looked for water they found none, and told the king. The king told them to see if they could find any snakes on the island; and when they found one, they brought it to him. He told them to put the snake close to the fire to make it hot and exhaust it and make it as thirsty as possible. Then a thread was tied to its tail, and the snake was released. It slithered away quickly, and the thread unwound from the ball. The men followed the snake until it dived into the ground. The king told them to dig there for water; they did so, and found plenty for all their needs.

King Harald now heard from his spies that King Svein had arrived at the mouth of the fjord with a large fleet; but it was taking them a long time to enter the fjord, because only one ship could pass through the channel at a time.

King Harald sailed his ships farther up the fjord to its widest point, to a place called Livobredning; at the far end of the creek there, only a narrow neck of land separates the fjord from the North Sea. Harald and his men rowed there that evening; and during the night, under cover of darkness, they unloaded their ships and dragged them across the isthmus. Then they loaded the ships again, and were all ready to sail before dawn. As they sailed north past Jutland they chanted:

> *Harald's slipped*
> *From Svein's grip!*

King Harald said that the next time he came to Denmark he was going to have a larger force and bigger ships.

The king then went north to Trondelag.

59. Preparations for war

THAT winter King Harald was in residence in Trondheim; and that same winter he had a ship built at Eyrar. It was much broader than normal warships; it was of the same size and proportions as the *Long Serpent*, and most carefully built in every detail.[1] Its prow had a dragon's head, and the stern had a dragon's tail, and the bows were inlaid with gold. It had thirty-five pairs of rowing-benches, with plenty of space between each; it was indeed a magnificent vessel. The king had all the fittings of the ship made with the utmost care, the sails and rigging as well as the anchor and ropes.

That winter, King Harald sent word south to King Svein in Denmark challenging him to come north to the Gota River in the spring to meet him in battle, to settle their dispute once and for all and decide which one of them should be king of both countries.

60. Harald goes south

THAT winter King Harald raised a full levy throughout Norway; and when spring came, a huge army assembled. He had the big ship launched into the River Nid, and the dragon emblems fitted to it. Then the poet Thjodolf said:

> I watched the ship, my lady,
> Launched down river to the ocean;
> See where the great longship
> Proudly lies at anchor.
> Above the prow, the dragon
> Rears its glowing head;
> The bows were bound with gold
> After the hull was launched.

King Harald then fitted out his ship, and when all was ready he steered it out of the river. His men rowed in fine style. In the words of the poet Thjodolf:

> One Saturday, King Harald
> Hauled down the long deck-awnings,

1. The *Long Serpent* was the name of the celebrated longship built by King Olaf Tryggvason (995–1000), 'the best-fitted and costliest ship ever built in Norway', according to Snorri Sturluson.

And Trondheim women proudly
Watched the ship glide past.
The young sea-king was steering
His new ship down the Nid,
While battle-hungry warriors
Dipped oars into the water.

As one, King Harald's warriors
Lift long oars from the ocean;
The womenfolk stand watching,
Wondering at their sea-skill.
We shall row, my lady, without tiring,
Till the black-tarred oars are broken,
Or the broad blades lie idle
When trumpets sound for battle.

Men will quake with terror
Before the seventy sea-oars
Are given deserved respite
From the labours of the ocean.
Norwegian arms are driving
This iron-studded dragon
Down the storm-tossed river
Like an eagle with wings flapping.

Harald sailed south along the coast with his full army of men and ships. As they were making their way east into Oslo Fjord a fierce storm blew up, and the fleet had to scatter for shelter in various havens, in the lee of the outlying islands and inside the fjords. In the words of the poet Thjodolf:

Polished prows of longships
Hug the wooded coastlines;
The army leader encloses
Norway with war-vessels.
Fighting troops are lying
In every creek and skerry;
Shield-protected warships
Shelter in lee of the land.

In the great storm that raged over them, the big ship needed good anchorage. In the words of the poet Thjodolf:

The king lashed the swollen
Sea with his dragon prow;
The great ship was heaving
Against the straining cables.
Storms wrenched at the iron
Anchor with cruel fingers;
Raging winds and boulders
Gnawed at the new-cast metal.

As soon as the weather was favourable, King Harald sailed with his army east to the Gota River, and arrived there in the evening. In the words of the poet Thjodolf:

Bravely has Harald fulfilled
His part of the bargain;
Norway's king is spending
This night at the kingdoms' border.
Harald keeps tryst with King Svein
At the appointed meeting-place,
A tryst to please the ravens –
Unless the Danes take fright.

61. Battle array

WHEN the Danes heard that the Norwegian army had arrived, all those who could tried to escape. The Norwegians learned that the Danish king also had his fleet out, and was lying with his army to the south off Fyn Island and the Smalands. When King Harald realized that King Svein was not going to keep his appointment for battle, as had been agreed, he did the same as he had done before: he sent back all the farmers' levy, keeping only 150 ships.

With this force he sailed south along Halland, raiding far and wide. He sailed into Laholms Fjord and plundered there also. But a little later King Svein came upon them with the Danish army, 300 ships in all. When the Norwegians saw this Danish host, King Harald called his army together with a trumpet blast. Some of his men said it would be better to flee, since it was hopeless to fight.

King Harald said, 'Sooner than flee, we shall all lie dead in heaps.' In the words of the poet Stein Herdisarson:

> *Eagle-hearted Harald*
> *Urged his men to battle;*
> *No hope of peace he offered*
> *To Norway's sturdy seamen.*
> *Norway's famous war-king*
> *Charged them to die nobly*
> *And not to think of yielding;*
> *His men then seized their weapons.*

King Harald drew up his fleet in battle-array, placing his own great dragon-ship forward in the centre of the line. In the words of the poet Thjodolf:

> *Open-handed Harald,*
> *Who feeds the wolves with corpses,*
> *Placed his greedy dragon-ship*
> *Foremost in line of battle.*

His ship had a large number of picked men on board; in the words of the poet Thjodolf:

> *Battle-eager Harald*
> *Bade his crew be steadfast;*
> *Warriors made a bulwark*
> *Of shields along the gunwales.*
> *The doughty king of Norway*
> *Lined his dragon longship*
> *With a wall of living shields;*
> *No foe could find a gap there.*

Marshal Ulf brought his ship alongside the royal vessel and told his men to keep the ship well to the fore. Stein Herdisarson was on board Ulf's ship, and said:

Ulf, King Harald's marshal,
Called upon our courage
When the long spears quivered
And men rowed into battle.
The king's loyal comrade
Urged us to go forward
And keep station beside the king;
And all his men agreed.

Earl Hakon Ivarsson lay on the outer flank of one wing with several ships, all excellently manned. At the far end of the other wing were the leaders of the Trondelag men, who also had a large and handsome force.

62. Ready for battle

KING SVEIN also drew up his ships in battle array and placed his own ship opposite King Harald's ship in the middle of the line, with Finn Arnason beside him; and next to them the Danes deployed all their best equipped and bravest forces. Then, on both sides, all the ships in the centre of the battle-lines were roped together. But since the fleets were so huge, there were still a great many ships left over, and their captains were free to bring their ships as far forward as they felt inclined – and that differed a lot.

Although the difference in odds was very great, both armies were extremely formidable. King Svein had six earls in his army. In the words of the poet Stein Herdisarson:

Fearlessly, King Harald
Faced his foes in battle;
With a hundred and fifty longships
He awaited the Danish onslaught.
Now the king of Denmark,
Eager to cross weapons,
Comes plunging over the ocean
With three hundred warships.

63. The Battle of the Nissa[1]

KING HARALD sounded the call to arms as soon as his ships were ready, and ordered his men to row forward. In the words of the poet Stein Herdisarson:

> Svein and Harald battled
> At the mouth of Nissa River;
> Both kings stood unyielding,
> For Harald asked no quarter.
> Norway's sword-girt warriors
> Rowed hard, just off Halland;
> Fiery wounds were gaping,
> Blood gushed into the ocean.

Battle was joined, and the fighting was very fierce as each king urged on his men. In the words of the poet Stein Herdisarson:

> The two great war-leaders,
> Shieldless, shunning armour,
> Called for thrust and parry;
> Armies were locked in battle.
> Stones and arrows were flying,
> Sword-blades were dyed crimson;
> All around, doomed warriors
> Fell before the onslaught.

It was late in the afternoon when the armies clashed, and the battle continued all night. King Harald wielded his bow for hours on end. In the words of the poet Thjodolf:

> Norway's king was bending
> His bow throughout that night,
> Raining a shower of arrows
> On the white shields of Denmark.

1. The battle at the mouth of the River Nissa was fought on 9 August 1062. The Nissa is in Halland (now part of Sweden), north of Skaane.

Bloody spear-points opened
Holes in iron armour;
Shields were pierced by arrows
From Harald's deadly dragon.

Earl Hakon and his company did not rope their ships together, but rowed against the Danish ships that were also lying free, and he cleared every ship he could grapple. When the Danes saw what was happening they all tried to withdraw their ships from Earl Hakon's path; but Earl Hakon went after them as they fell back, until they were on the point of being routed. At that moment a small skiff came rowing up to Earl Hakon's ship and hailed him, telling him that one of the Norwegian flanks was giving way and that many of the king's men there had been killed. So the earl rowed over to that part of the battle and attacked so fiercely there that the Danes were once again forced to fall back.

Earl Hakon kept this up all night, holding his ships at the outskirts of the battle and making sorties to wherever the need was greatest; and wherever he attacked, nothing could withstand him.

Towards the end of the night the main force of the Danish fleet broke into flight, when King Harald and his men boarded King Svein's ship and cleared it so completely that everyone on board was killed, except for those who jumped overboard. In the words of Arnor the Earls'-Poet:

Brave King Svein of Denmark
I am sure had every reason
To leave his stricken longship;
Steel bit hard on helmets.
The royal ship lay empty
When Denmark's quick-tongued leader
Leapt from the bloodied gunwales,
Leaving his fallen comrades.

When King Svein's banner had fallen and his ship had been cleared, all the rest of his army took to flight and many were killed. The men on the ships that had been roped together jumped overboard, and some of them managed to get aboard the other ships that had been loose. And all Svein's men who could still do so, now rowed away.

The loss of life was very great; and where the kings themselves had been fighting and the centres of the fleets had been roped together, more than seventy of King Svein's ships were left lying empty. In the words of the poet Thjodolf:

> *It's said that at least seventy*
> *Of Denmark's finest longships*
> *Were cleared in a few moments*
> *By the tireless king of Norway.*

King Harald rowed after the Danes and pursued them, but this was by no means easy, for the fjord was so crowded with ships that it was difficult to get past them.

Earl Finn Arnason, whose eyesight was very poor, refused to flee and was taken prisoner. In the words of the poet Thjodolf:

> *Svein could not gain victory*
> *With six earls in his army,*
> *Despite their proven courage,*
> *Eager for the battle.*
> *Warlike Earl Finn Arnason,*
> *Too proud to flee the fighting,*
> *Refused to try to escape,*
> *And at last was taken captive.*

64. Disguise

EARL HAKON stayed behind with his ship while King Harald and the rest of the army were pursuing the fleeing Danes, because the earl's ship could not get past the vessels which lay in the way.

Then a stranger came rowing up to the earl's ship in a small boat and lay to under the fo'c'sle; he was a tall man, wearing a broad cowl. He shouted up to the ship, 'Where is the earl?'

Earl Hakon was for'ard, trying to staunch a wounded man's bleeding. He glanced towards the hooded man and asked him his name.

The man said, 'This is Vandrad here; I want to have a word with you.' [1]

Earl Hakon leaned out over the gunwale towards him. The stranger continued, 'I would accept my life from you, if you wished to grant me it.'

The earl stood up and called two of his men who were close friends of his. 'Step into the boat and take Vandrad ashore,' he told them. 'Then escort him to my friend Karl, the farmer. As a token, ask Karl to lend Vandrad the horse I gave him the other day, and tell him also to provide his own saddle, and his son as an escort.'

They stepped into the boat and started rowing, with Vandrad at the helm. It was just before dawn, and the fjord was teeming with ships on the move, some heading for land and others out to sea, ships both large and small. Vandrad threaded his way between the ships where the gaps were widest; but whenever any Norwegian vessels came close, Earl Hakon's friends gave their names and were then allowed to go on their way. Vandrad steered along the coast for a while, and did not try to land until they were well past the fleet.

It was beginning to grow light as they walked up to Karl's farm. They went into the living-room and found Karl there; he had just got up. The earl's men gave him their message. Karl said they must first have something to eat, and had a table laid for them and brought them a basin for washing.

Karl's wife then came into the room and said, 'How extraordinary! We couldn't sleep a wink all night for all that screaming and shouting!'

1. The name Vandrad occurs elsewhere in Icelandic saga literature as an ilias; it means 'one who is in trouble'. The author is careful not to reveal Vandrad's identity here; but his readers, knowing the convention, would know that something was afoot. (Cf. chapters 67–9).

'Didn't you know that kings have been fighting all night?' said Karl.

'And who won, then?' she asked.

'The Norwegians won,' said Karl.

'Our king must have fled again, as usual,' she said.

'No one knows whether he has fled or fallen,' said Karl.

'What a wretched king we have,' said the woman. 'He not only walks with a limp, but he's a coward as well.'

Then Vandrad said, 'I don't think the king is a coward; but he hasn't much victory luck.'

Vandrad was the last to wash his hands, and afterwards he dried them on the middle part of the towel. The woman of the house snatched the towel away from him and said, 'How uncouth you are! It's boorish to wet the towel all over at the same time.'

Karl now invited them to the table, and Vandrad sat in the middle. They took their time over eating, and then went outside. The horse was ready, and the farmer's son was waiting to accompany him with another horse. The two of them rode away into the forest, while the earl's men walked down to their boat and rowed back to the earl's ship.

65. The spoils

KING HARALD and his men pursued the fleeing Danes only a short way, and then turned back to the empty ships and searched among the slain. On King Svein's ship they found a great number of corpses, but not the body of the king himself; they assumed, however, that he must be dead.

King Harald had the corpses of his own men prepared for burial, and the wounds of the injured seen to. Then he had the bodies of Svein's men taken ashore, and sent word to the farmers there to bury them.

After that he shared out the spoils.

He stayed there for some time. Then he was told the news

that King Svein had reached Zealand and that all the troops that had escaped from the battle had flocked back to him, and a great number of others besides; so King Svein now had a huge army with him.

66. The captive

EARL FINN ARNASON was taken prisoner in the battle, as was said before, and was led before King Harald. The king was in a very cheerful mood.

'So we meet again, Finn!' he said. 'The last time was in Norway. These Danish courtiers have not stood very firmly by your side. The Norwegians now have the unpleasant task of dragging a blind man like you behind them in order to keep you alive.'

Earl Finn replied, 'The Norwegians have many unpleasant duties to perform, but none so bad as your own orders.'

'Do you want your life spared, however little you deserve it?' asked the king.

'Not by you, dog!' said the earl.

'Would you rather that your kinsman Magnus gave you your life?' asked the king. Harald's son, Magnus, was then in charge of one of the Norwegian ships.[1]

The earl said, 'How can that puppy grant anyone his life?'

The king laughed, and found it amusing to tease him. So he went on, 'Will you then accept your life from your niece Thora?'

'Is she here?' asked the earl.

'Yes, she's here,' said King Harald.

It was then that Earl Finn uttered the insult that has long been remembered as showing how angry he was, since he could not curb his tongue: 'No wonder you fought so lustily, if the mare was with you.'

Earl Finn's life was spared, and King Harald kept him with

1. Magnus was the son of King Harald and Thora, who was Earl Finn's niece (cf. chapter 45).

him for a while. Finn was always in a black mood, and surly in his replies.

Finally King Harald said, 'I can see, Finn, that you have no desire to make friends with me or your kinsmen. I will now give you leave to go back to your King Svein.'

Earl Finn replied, 'I accept your offer – and the sooner I get away from here, the more grateful I'll be.'

The king had the earl and his followers ferried ashore, where they were well received by the people of Halland.

King Harald sailed north with his army to Norway. He landed first at Oslo, and there he gave home leave to all who wanted it.

67. Karl's reward

IT is said that King Svein stayed that winter in Denmark enjoying the same power in his kingdom as he had before. During the winter he sent messengers north to Halland to fetch Karl and his wife. When they arrived at the royal court, the king summoned Karl to his presence, and asked whether he recognized him or thought he had ever seen him before.

Karl said, 'I recognize you now, sire, and I recognized you then, as soon as I saw you. May God be praised that the little help I gave you was of some use to you.'

King Svein said, 'For the rest of my life I shall remain in your debt. And now, in the first place, I am going to give you any farm in Zealand you wish to choose; and secondly I shall make you into a great man if you prove able enough.'

Karl thanked the king handsomely for these words; then he said, 'But there is still one favour I should like to ask of you.'

The king asked what it was.

'I want to ask you, sire, to allow me to take my wife with me,' said Karl.

The king said, 'That is one favour I am not going to grant you. Instead, I shall find you a much wiser and better woman for a wife. Your present wife can keep your old croft in Halland, and she can support herself on that.'

The king gave Karl a magnificent farm and found him an excellent wife, and Karl became a man of considerable stature. The story spread far and wide, and news of it reached Norway.

68. Jealousy

KING HARALD was in residence at Oslo during the winter after the Battle of the Nissa. That autumn, when the army came back from Denmark, there was a tremendous amount of talk and story-telling about the battle, for everyone who had taken part in it felt he had something worth telling about it.

On one occasion some of them were sitting in a cellar drinking and being very talkative. They were talking about the battle of the Nissa, and arguing about who had achieved the most fame there. They all agreed that no one there had been the equal of Earl Hakon: 'He was the bravest in battle and also the shrewdest. And he had the greatest luck, for everything he did was so effective. It was he who won the victory.'

King Harald had been outside in the courtyard, talking with some of his men. Now he walked to the door of the cellar and said, 'Everyone here now wants to be called Hakon.'

And with that he went away.

69. The secret revealed

EARL HAKON went to the Uplands in the autumn and stayed there over the winter in his own domains. He was immensely popular with all the Uplanders.

One day late next spring, when his men were sitting and drinking, they started once again to argue about the Battle of the Nissa. They were all full of praise for Earl Hakon, but there were some who mentioned other names as well. When they had argued the matter for a while, one of them said, 'It may well be that Earl Hakon was not the only man who fought bravely at the Battle of the Nissa, but no one, in my opinion, had the same share of luck as he had.'

The others replied that his greatest luck was to have put so many Danes to flight.

The man said, 'It was even greater luck when he saved King Svein's life.'

Someone rebuked him and said, 'You don't know what you're talking about.'

'Oh, yes, I do,' he replied, 'because one of the men who ferried King Svein ashore told me so himself.'

And now, as so often happens, the old saying came true that 'a king has many ears', for the story was brought to King Harald. And as soon as he heard it, he had a number of horses fetched, and set off that same night with two hundred men. They rode all night and the following day. Then a number of farmers came riding towards them on their way to market with flour and malt.

One of the king's companions was a man called Gamal. He rode up to one of the farmers he knew and took him aside for a talk.

'I will pay you well,' said Gamal, 'if you ride as fast as you can by all the secret short-cuts you know, and go straight to Earl Hakon. Tell him that the king is planning to kill him, for he has now found out that it was Earl Hakon who smuggled King Svein ashore at the Nissa.'

They agreed on the payment, and the farmer now rode all the way to the earl's house. The earl was up late, drinking, and had not yet gone to bed. The farmer gave him the message, and the earl got to his feet at once with all his men. He had all the valuables taken from the house and hidden in the wood, and everyone had left the house before the king arrived later that night. The king stayed there for the rest of the night, but Earl Hakon rode all the way east to Sweden to King Steinkel,[1] and stayed with him throughout the summer.

King Harald went back home to Oslo. In the summer he

1. King Steinkel was king of Sweden from *c.* 1056 to 1066.

went north to Trondheim and stayed there until the autumn, when he returned to Oslo.

70. Taxes and dues

EARL HAKON went back to the Uplands in the summer as soon as he heard that King Harald had gone north, and stayed there until the king came back south again. Then the earl went east to Varmland and spent most of the winter there; King Steinkel put him in charge of that province.

But late in the winter, Earl Hakon travelled west to Romerike with a large force which the Gotalanders and the Varmlanders had given him. He collected his estate-dues and taxes from the Uplanders, and then went back to Gotaland and stayed there over the spring.

King Harald spent the winter in Oslo, and sent men to the Uplands to collect there the taxes and land-dues, and the king's fines. But the Uplanders said that they would willingly pay all their lawful taxes and dues – but only to Earl Hakon, for as long as he was alive and had forfeited neither his rights nor his earldom. So the king got no land-dues from the Uplands that winter.

71. Peace treaty

THAT winter, messages were exchanged between Norway and Denmark, and it was agreed that the Norwegians and Danes wanted to make a peace treaty between the two countries, and they urged their kings to bring this about. There were conciliatory exchanges, and eventually a peace meeting between King Harald and King Svein was arranged at the Gota River.

In the spring both sides assembled a huge force of men and ships for the meeting. The poet has described the kings' journeys in his poem :[1]

1. The name of this poet is not known.

The warlike king of Denmark
Girds his realm with longships
North all the way to Oresund;
King Svein is leaving harbour.
Golden beaks of warships
Are ploughing deep furrows
In the ocean west of Halland;
The spray-boards quiver.

Oath-keeping King Harald
Spikes the seas with warships;
Svein carves the ocean,
Sailing to a royal meeting.
Svein, the friend of ravens,
Lord of the Danish sea-ways,
Sails to meet King Harald
With a host of Danish warriors.

It is stated there that these kings held the meeting which had been arranged for them. The meeting took place at the border of their kingdoms, as this stanza attests:

South you sailed, great Harald,
At Denmark's invitation;
The reason for this meeting
Was no less urgent than before.
The Danish king is heading
Northwards to the border,
Hoping to meet King Harald;
Gales lash the ocean.

As soon as the kings met, discussions about terms began. But no sooner had the negotiations started than people started listing the losses they had sustained from all the fighting and plundering and killing. This went on for a long time, as the poet has said:

Worthy farmers argued
Loudly at the meeting;

Bitter words could only
Rouse the rage of others.
Men who always quarrel
Have no wish for treaties;
Royal pride was offended,
Anger rose between them.

Royal anger swelling
Could put an end to peace-talks;
Men of mediation
Weighed the matter wisely.
Kings want to be certain
What their men are wanting;
Greed alone is the reason
Why peace is not concluded.

Then the best and wisest men intervened, and a treaty was finally concluded between the two kings; the terms were that King Harald was to have Norway and King Svein was to have Denmark, recognizing the ancient boundaries between the two countries. Neither of the kings was to pay compensation to the other. The war between them was to cease, and each side was to keep whatever gains the fighting had brought them. This peace treaty was to remain in force for as long as they both were kings; and the treaty was sealed with binding oaths. After that the kings exchanged hostages. In the words of the poet:

I have heard how Harald
And Svein exchanged gladly
Hostages for peace;
That was God's will.
May they honour their pledges
And keep the peace inviolate,
Sacred to both their nations;
It was sealed before witnesses.

King Harald now went back north to Norway with his army, and King Svein returned south to Denmark.

72. Battle with Earl Hakon

KING HARALD spent the summer at Oslo, and sent his men to the Uplands to collect the dues and taxes he was owed there. The farmers, however, refused to make any payments, and said they were keeping everything for Earl Hakon until such time as he returned; Earl Hakon was in Gotaland with a large force at that time.

Late that summer, King Harald sailed south to Konungahella, and as soon as he arrived there he assembled all the light skiffs he could get and travelled up the Gota river. The boats had to be hauled overland at every waterfall they came to, and by this means they brought the boats to Lake Vaner. They rowed east across the lake to the other side, where the king had heard that Earl Hakon was to be found. When the earl got news of the king's arrival, he came down from the hills to meet him, because he did not want the king to plunder there. Earl Hakon had a large force that the Gotalanders had given him.

King Harald brought his ships into the mouth of a river, and then disembarked his forces, leaving some of his men behind to guard the ships. The king himself and a few others were on horseback, but most of his troops were on foot. They had to pass through a wood, and then cross some bogs overgrown with brushwood before coming to a low hill. When they reached the hill they caught sight of Earl Hakon's forces on the far side of yet another bog. Both sides now formed up.

The king told his men to wait up on the hillside; 'Let us first see whether they are going to launch an attack on us. Hakon is a very impetuous man.'

It was a frosty day, with light snow showers. Harald and his men sheltered under their shields, but the Gotalanders were only lightly clad, and soon began to feel the cold.

Earl Hakon told them to wait for the king to attack first, so that they would be fighting on level ground. Earl Hakon had the banner that had belonged to King Magnus the Good.

The Lawman of Gotaland, a man called Thorvid, was sitting

on a horse which was tethered to a peg driven into the spongy ground. He spoke up and said, 'God knows that we have a large force here, and all of them brave warriors. Let us ensure that King Steinkel can be told that we have supported this good earl well. I know that if the Norwegians attack us, we will face up to them with courage; but if the younger men get restive and will not wait, we must run no farther than this brook. And if the young men get even more restive, which I am sure won't happen, we must run no farther than that mound.'

At that very moment the Norwegians all jumped to their feet, roaring their war-cries and beating their shields. The Gotaland army also started to yell. The Lawman's horse was startled by all the shouting, and pulled hard at its tether; the peg was jerked out of the ground and struck the Lawman on the head.

'Damn your Norwegians' hands for that!' he cried, and galloped away.

King Harald had previously warned his men: 'Even though we shout and make a din, we must not move down off the hillside until they come and attack us.' They did as he ordered.

As soon as the war-cry was raised, Earl Hakon had his banner moved forward; but when the Gotalanders advanced to the hill, the Norwegians came sweeping down on them. Many of the earl's men were killed at once, and some of them fled. The Norwegians did not pursue the fleeing men very far, for it was already evening. They captured Earl Hakon's banner there, and all the weapons and equipment they could lay their hands on.

On their way back, King Harald had both the standards carried before him. They were discussing whether or not Earl Hakon had been killed. Going through the wood they could only move in single file; suddenly a man rushed out on to the path and thrust a spear through the man who was carrying Earl Hakon's banner. The stranger then grabbed the banner and darted back into the wood with it. When the king was told about this, he said, 'The earl is still alive! Bring me my armour!'

The king rode on through the night down to his ships. Some of his men felt that the earl had amply avenged himself; but the poet Thjodolf said:

> King Steinkel's Swedish warriors
> Were to help the brave Earl Hakon;
> But mighty Harald's warriors
> Sent them straight to Hell.
> Hakon fled in panic,
> Forsaken by his allies;
> Yet some men try to praise him
> For running from the battle.

King Harald spent the rest of the night at his ships. In the morning when it grew light, the river was frozen over so hard that one could walk on the ice right round the ships. The king told his men to cut a channel through the ice from the ships down to the lake; they set to work at once hacking a way through the ice.

King Harald's son, Magnus, was in command of the ship farthest down the river and nearest the lake. When they had almost completed the channel through the ice, a man came running across to where they were working and started hacking at the ice like a madman.

Someone said: 'It's always the same: there's no one like Hall Kodran's-Killer. Just look at him cutting through that ice!'

There was a man on board Magnus's ship called Thormod Eindridason. As soon as he heard the name 'Kodran's-Killer' he rushed up to this man Hall and struck him dead.[1] Thormod Eindridason had been a year old when his kinsman Kodran

---

1. *This Kodran was the son of Gudmund Eyjolfsson the Power-ful; and Gudmund's sister was Valgerd, the mother of Jorunn, the mother of Thormod Eindridason.*

This curious little episode is also described in *Ljosvetninga Saga*, and may have been borrowed from *Hakon Ivarsson's Saga*, of which only fragments and a Latin summary have survived.

Gudmund the Powerful was an ancestor of Snorri Sturluson. He is one of the chief characters in *Ljosvetninga Saga*, and appears in many other sagas, including *Njal's Saga*.

had been killed, and he had never seen his killer, Hall Otryggsson, before this moment.

By this time the channel to the lake had been completed; so Magnus brought his ship out of the river, hoisted sail, and headed west across the lake. The king's ship had been farthest up the river, so he was the last to get out of the ice. Hall Otryggsson had been one of his own men and was very dear to him, so the king was furious over the killing; but by the time the king reached harbour it was getting very late, and Magnus had already smuggled the killer away into the woods. Magnus offered to pay compensation on his behalf, but even so the king was on the point of attacking Magnus and his crew when their friends intervened and brought about a reconciliation.

73. Punitive measures

THAT winter King Harald went up to Romerike with a large army, and brought charges against the farmers for withholding their dues and taxes, and supporting his enemies in rebellion against him. So the king had the farmers seized; some of them he ordered to be maimed, others killed, and most of them deprived of all their possessions. All those who could escape fled. He had many districts burned and laid completely waste. In the words of the poet Thjodolf :

> The hammer of Denmark's armies
> Gave Romerike rough treatment;
> Harald's gallant warriors
> Crushed all opposition.
> Fires blazed in punishment –
> Harald's retribution;
> Flames cured the peasants
> Of disloyalty to Harald.

Then King Harald went up to Heidmark and razed many districts there as well, causing no less destruction than he had in Romerike. From there he went to Hadaland and out to

Ringerike, which he also burned and ravaged. In the words of
the poet Thjodolf:

> Flames gnawed the roof-trees
> Of Harald's stubborn subjects;
> Thus King Harald punished
> The wayward men of Heidmark.
> Peasants begged for mercy,
> But flames pronounced the verdict;
> The sentences meant suffering
> Before the fires abated.

After this the farmers submitted to the king completely.

74. Retrospect

FROM the death of King Magnus until the Battle of the Nissa
fifteen years had passed, and then another two years went by
before King Harald and King Svein made their treaty. In the
words of the poet Thjodolf:

> At long last, fierce King Harald
> Turned keen swords into ploughshares;
> Weapons had maimed shields at sea;
> In the third year, peace was made.

After this treaty was made, King Harald's dispute with the
Uplanders lasted for a year and a half. In the words of the poet
Thjodolf:

> No poet can with justice
> Describe the royal vengeance
> That left the Uplands farmsteads
> Derelict and empty.
> In eighteen months, King Harald
> Earned himself renown;
> His acts will be remembered
> Until the end of time.

75. England

EDWARD ÆTHELREDSSON [Edward the Confessor] was king of England after his half-brother Harda-Knut. He was nicknamed Edward the Good, which describes him well.[1]

King Edward's mother was Queen Emma, the daughter of Duke Richard of Normandy; and her brother was Duke Robert, the father of William the Bastard, who was then Duke of Normandy at Rouen.[2]

King Edward [the Confessor] was married to Queen Edith, the daughter of Earl Godwin Wulfnothsson.[3]

1. Edward the Confessor was king of England from June 1042 to January 1066. He was the son of Æthelred the Unready. After being brought up at the ducal court of Normandy, he succeeded his half-brother Harda-Knut, the son of Knut Sveinsson (Canute the Great); Harda-Knut had been abroad on the death of his father in November 1035 and did not succeed to the throne of England until 1040.

2. Emma was the illegitimate daughter of Richard I (Richard the Fearless), Duke of Normandy; and Duke Robert the Magnificent was her nephew, not her brother, as the saga states. Emma became the second wife (in 1002) of King Æthelred the Unready of England, and their sons were Alfred the Ætheling and Edward the Confessor. In 1017 she was married to Knut Sveinsson, who was even then trying to forestall any Norman designs on the English throne; their son was Harda-Knut.

William the Bastard was the seventh Duke of Normandy, a descendant of the first Duke, Rollo (the Norwegian Viking Hrolf the Ganger, so called because he was so huge that no horse could carry him and he had to walk). Rollo captured and ruled Rouen late in the ninth century, and was eventually granted Normandy by King Charles the Simple of France in 911. William was the illegitimate son of Robert the Magnificent and a girl called Herleve, daughter of a Falaise tanner; he was born in 1027 or 1028, and succeeded to the duchy in 1035. It was not until 1054, after long years of rebellion and war, that he finally established his authority.

3. Earl Godwin of Wessex was one of the most powerful men in England in the first half of the eleventh century. A self-made man,

Edith's brothers were Earl Tostig (who was the eldest), Earl Morcar, Earl Waltheof, Earl Svein, and Harold, who was the youngest.[1]

Harold had been brought up at King Edward's court, and was the king's foster-son. The king loved him dearly as if he were his own son, for the king had no children of his own.[2]

76. Visit to Normandy

ONE summer, Harold Godwinsson had to go to Wales. He went by ship; but once they had sailed they ran into bad weather and

---

he was created an earl by King Knut by 1018, and married Gyda (English Edith), the sister of Knut's brother-in-law, Earl Ulf (the father of King Svein Ulfsson of Denmark, cf. chapter 18). When Earl Godwin died in 1053, shortly after returning from brief exile, the house of Godwin was established as one of the most powerful dynasties in England.

1. The saga is inaccurate here. Earl Godwin had six sons, not five. Svein was the eldest, and died in 1052; then, in order of age, Harold (born c. 1022), Tostig, Gyrth, Leofwin, and Wulfnoth. Leofwin and Gyrth were both killed at the Battle of Hastings with Harold. Tostig was appointed Earl of Northumbria in 1055, and Harold succeeded his father as Earl of Wessex in 1053.

Morcar was the son of Earl Ælfgar of Mercia, and became Earl of Northumbria in 1065 when the Northumbrians expelled Earl Tostig.

Waltheof was the son of Earl Siward of Northumbria (cf. chapter 84).

2. This is highly unlikely, for Harold was about twenty years old when Edward the Confessor came to the throne in 1042. Despite the fact that he was King Edward's brother-in-law, his relations with the king were often strained; he was exiled with his father, Earl Godwin, for a year in 1051. After he succeeded to the earldom in 1053, however, his services to the king as a military commander were invaluable, and he gradually became the most powerful man in England, overshadowing his ascetic king.

were driven out into the open sea. They managed to make land in Normandy after a most perilous storm.

They made their way to Rouen and went to see Duke William. The duke gave Harold and his companions a most cordial welcome, and Harold stayed there throughout the autumn and was entertained most hospitably. The bad weather continued for a long time, and the sea was too rough for crossing; and as winter approached, the duke and Harold agreed that Harold should stay there until spring.

Harold used to sit on the high-seat on one side of the duke, and on the duke's other side sat the duchess; she was the loveliest woman people had ever seen.[1] The three of them always had a good time, drinking together; Duke William was usually the first to go to bed, but Harold used to stay up late into the night, talking with the duchess. This went on for most of the winter.

Then on one occasion when the two of them were talking together, she said to Harold, 'The duke has been speaking to me, and asking me what we are always talking about; he is beginning to get angry.'

Harold said, 'Then we must let him know at once what all our conversations have been about.'

Next day Harold went to see the duke, and they went into the audience-chamber, where the duchess and all his counsellors were waiting.

Harold said, 'I must first inform you, sir, that there was more to my coming here than I have already told you: I wish to ask for the hand of your daughter in marriage. I have talked about this a great deal with her mother, and she has promised to support me in this proposal.'

As soon as Harold had made this known, it was well received by all those present, and they pleaded the case with the duke.

1. Duke William's wife was Matilda, the daughter of Count Baldwin of Flanders. Her chief physical attribute was her remarkably small size; in 1961 her remains were disinterred at Caen, and proved that she could not have been more than an inch or two over four feet tall (William seems to have been about five feet ten inches tall). She bore him four sons and five or six daughters.

Finally the girl was betrothed to Harold, but since she was still very young, it was agreed that the wedding should be postponed for a few years.[1]

77. A new king

IN the spring, Harold made his ship ready and sailed away. He and the duke parted on the friendliest terms. Harold went back to England to the court of King Edward; he never returned to Normandy to claim his bride.

King Edward was king over England for twenty-three years, and died in London on the fifth of January. He was buried in St Paul's Cathedral, and is regarded as a saint by the English.[2]

At that time, Earl Godwin's sons were the most powerful men in England. Tostig had been made commander of the English army, and he was put in charge of the nation's defences when the king began to grow old. Earl Tostig had authority over all the other earls in England. His brother, Harold, was always

1. There is no suggestion in English sources that Harold was ever betrothed to William's daughter, Agatha; but there seems to be no doubt at all that Harold visited William in Normandy, probably in the year 1064. English and Norman sources all agree that on this occasion, Harold swore some kind of oath to William, vividly commemorated in the Bayeux Tapestry. This oath was widely regarded as a pledge to support William's claim to the English throne, or at least not to oppose it. Harold seems to have gone to the Continent on some mission, but was storm-driven to Ponthieu, where he was arrested by the local count and imprisoned at Beaurain. One of his men managed to escape, however, and brought word to William, who was then overlord of the area. William had Harold released; and Harold stayed with him for some time, and took part in military expeditions with him.

2. King Edward died in London on 5 January 1066, after an illness that lasted for a few weeks. He was buried the following day, not in St Paul's Cathedral but in St Peter's Church (the original name for Westminster Abbey) which he had founded and which was consecrated only eight days before his death.

next in precedence to him at court, and was in charge of the royal exchequer.[1]

It is said that as the king's death was drawing near, Harold was beside him, and only a few other people were present. Harold is supposed to have bent down over the king, and then said, 'I name you all as witnesses that the king has just given me the crown and whole kingdom of England.'

Then the king was lifted dead from his bed.

That same day a meeting of the witan was held to consider the succession to the throne. Harold called upon his witnesses to testify that King Edward on his dying day had given him the kingdom. The outcome of the meeting was that Harold was made king, and was crowned and consecrated in St Paul's Cathedral on the sixth of January. All the chieftains and all the people paid him their homage.[2]

When his brother, Earl Tostig, heard this he was extremely displeased, for he felt that he was no less entitled to the crown. 'I want the leaders of the land,' he said, 'to elect as king the man who, in their opinion, is best suited for the task.'

1. Tostig seems to have been King Edward's favourite, but there is no evidence that he wielded greater authority in England than Harold, who was his elder brother. Tostig had been appointed Earl of Northumbria in 1055 and was thus in charge of the kingdom's northern defences; and he helped Harold in the prolonged and ultimately successful campaign against King Gruffyd of Wales which established Harold as the greatest military leader in England. But in 1065, Tostig was expelled from his earldom by the Northumbrians and was outlawed from England.

2. Harold was probably crowned in Westminster Abbey, not St Paul's, on 6 January 1066, the same day as King Edward was buried.

It seems probable that towards the end of his life, King Edward granted the succession to Harold, although it was not strictly within his power to do so – kings were elected then. The political situation in England, threatened with the danger of invasion from Norway and Normandy, made it imperative to have a king of proven military ability and authority, and Harold's election seems to have been unanimous. One version of the *Anglo-Saxon Chronicle* says : 'He succeeded to the kingdom as the king granted it to him and as he was chosen thereto.'

The brothers exchanged messages and Harold said he refused to surrender his kingship since he had already been enthroned at the proper place and then anointed and crowned king. Most people gave Harold their support, and he was also in control of all the royal treasuries.

78. Tostig in Denmark

WHEN Harold realized that his brother Tostig wanted to deprive him of the throne, he lost all faith in him, for Tostig was a very shrewd and powerful man and had influential friends among the leaders of the country. King Harold therefore deprived Earl Tostig of the army command, and withdrew all the authority he had had over the other earls in the kingdom.

Earl Tostig could not endure being subservient to his own brother; so he went away with his force south across the Channel to Flanders, where he stayed for a short time before going to Frisia and from there on to Denmark to see his cousin, King Svein Ulfsson.[1]

The earl asked King Svein for his help and support; the king invited him to stay in Denmark and offered him an earldom there, which would make him a chieftain of considerable standing.

Earl Tostig replied, 'The only thing I want is to go back to my own estates in England; and if I can get no support from

1. *King Svein's father, Earl Ulf, was the brother of Earl Tostig's mother, Gyda.*

In actual fact, Tostig had been exiled from England several months before Harold came to the throne. He was expelled by the Northumbrians from his earldom in 1065, and went to Flanders then to take refuge with his wife's kinsman, Count Baldwin (Duke William's father-in-law). Tostig was already a threat to the security of England before Harold became king; he greatly resented the fact that at the time of his expulsion, in 1065, Harold had not come to his aid.

you for this, sire, my proposal would be to give you all the support I can muster in England if you are prepared to take a Danish army over to England to conquer it, as your uncle Knut once did.'

King Svein replied, 'I am so much a lesser man than my uncle, King Knut, that I can only just hold Denmark against the Norwegians. Old Knut got Denmark by inheritance and won England by conquest, and for a time it looked as if it might cost him his life. Then he gained Norway without any fighting at all. As far as I am concerned, I intend to be guided more by my own limitations than by my uncle Knut's achievements.'

Earl Tostig said, 'My visit here will have more meagre results than I had hoped from someone of your high position, considering how great is your kinsman's need. It looks now as if I shall have to look for friends in less likely quarters; but it may well be that I shall find a chieftain who is less reluctant than you, sire, to undertake great enterprises.'

With that they parted, and not on very friendly terms.[1]

79. Tostig in Norway

EARL TOSTIG now turned towards Norway and went to see King Harald Sigurdsson, who was then at Oslo Fjord. When they met, Earl Tostig explained what he had in mind, and told him everything about his journey since he left England. He

1. King Svein Ulfsson had claims of his own on the throne of England, as the successor of the Knut dynasty that had ruled Denmark and England. He also had a claim through King Magnus the Good of Norway, from whom he inherited Denmark (cf. chapter 28). King Magnus of Norway had made a treaty with Harda-Knut of Denmark, in 1038 or 1039, that if either of them should die without an heir, his kingdom should pass to the survivor. When Harda-Knut died in 1042, King Magnus claimed not only Denmark but England as well.

asked King Harald to give him support for his claim to the throne of England.

King Harald replied that the Norwegians would not be too eager to go over to England to make war and have an English commander over them. 'People say,' he added, 'that the English are not entirely to be trusted.'

Earl Tostig said, 'Is it true, as I heard in England, that your nephew King Magnus sent messengers to King Edward to tell him that both England and Denmark belonged to him, since he had inherited both countries from Harda-Knut, according to a sworn treaty between them?'

King Harald retorted, 'Then why didn't he claim both these countries, if they were his by right?'

'Why don't you hold Denmark now, as King Magnus did before you?' said the earl.

'The Danes have little cause to boast about their dealings with us Norwegians,' said King Harald. 'We have left our mark on those kinsmen of yours often enough.'

'If you will not tell me, then I shall tell you,' said Earl Tostig. 'King Magnus won all Denmark because the chieftains there all supported him; but you failed to win it because all the people there were against you. And King Magnus did not try to conquer England because all the people there wanted Edward as their king. But if you want to conquer England, I can ensure that the majority of the chieftains there will be your friends and give you support. Compared with my brother Harold, the only thing I lack is the title of king.

'Everyone knows that there has never been born in Scandinavia a warrior to compare with you; and it seems to me very strange that you should spend fifteen years trying to conquer Denmark, and yet be so reluctant to have England when it is yours for the taking.'

King Harald thought carefully over what the earl had said, and realized that there was a lot of truth in his words; and at the same time he had a great desire to win this kingdom.[1]

1. Harald of Norway had had designs on England for some time; he considered himself the proper heir to the treaty between King Magnus and King Harda-Knut. Welsh and Irish sources also sug-

After this, the earl and the king talked together often and at length; and finally they came to the decision to invade England that summer.

King Harald then sent word throughout Norway, raising a half-levy of the whole army. This was much talked about, and there was great speculation about the outcome of this venture. Some people reckoned up all King Harald's great achievements, and said that nothing would be too difficult for him; but there were others who said that England would be very hard to conquer – it was very populous, and the warriors who were known as the king's Housecarls were so valiant that any one of them was worth any two of the best men in King Harald's army.[1] Then Marshal Ulf said:

> Gladly I'd draw my sword
> Once more for my King Harald;
> But little use his marshals
> Would be on board his longship,
> If one of England's warriors
> Could deal with two Norwegians.
> When I was young, my lady,
> Things were different then.

Marshal Ulf died that same year. King Harald stood at his graveside, and as he walked away, he said, 'There lies the most loyal and trusty liegeman a lord ever had.'

In the spring, Earl Tostig sailed west to Flanders to meet the men who had accompanied him from England, and also the troops who had gathered to him since then from England and Flanders.

---

gest that in 1058, Harald's son, Magnus, attempted a conquest of England with a fleet drawn from Norway, Ireland, Orkney and Shetland.

1. The Royal Housecarls were a body of professional warriors, first instituted by King Knut the Great, and numbering perhaps 3,000. They were the core of the English army, well-disciplined and brave; their main weapon was the long-handled Danish bearded battle-axe. They were probably the finest troops in Europe at this time.

80. An omen

KING HARALD'S army assembled in the Solund Isles. When Harald was ready to leave Trondheim, he went to St Olaf's shrine and opened it, and trimmed the saint's hair and nails. Then he locked the shrine again and threw the key into the river Nid, and since then St Olaf's shrine has never been opened. Thirty-five years had passed by then since his death, and he had been thirty-five years old when he died.[1]

King Harald sailed south with his own men to meet the main army. A great host was gathered there, and it is said that King Harald had over two hundred ships, apart from supply-ships and smaller craft.[2]

While they were waiting at the Solund Isles, a man called Gyrdir, who was on board the king's ship, had a dream. He dreamed that he was on the king's ship looking up towards the island, where he could see a huge ogress standing with a big knife in one hand and a trough in the other. In his dream he could see right over the whole fleet, and on every prow he could see a bird squatting, all of them ravens or eagles. The ogress was chanting:

> Norway's warrior sea-king
> Has been enticed westward
> To fill England's graveyards;
> It's all to my advantage.
> Birds of carrion follow
> To feast on valiant seamen;
> They know there will be plenty,
> And I'll be there to help them.

1. The shrine was opened again in the reign of King Magnus Hakonarson (1263–80), but the last resting-place of the earthly remains of St Olaf is now unknown; they were buried in Trondheim in 1568, but the position of the grave is not marked.

2. With the reinforcements that King Harald was to gather in Scotland, it has been estimated that the Norwegian armada for the conquest of England numbered about 300 ships and 9,000 men.

81. Another omen

THERE was a man called Thord who was on board a vessel which lay close to the king's ship. One night he dreamed that he saw King Harald's fleet sailing towards land, and he knew that this was England. Ashore he could see a great battle array, and both armies then made ready for battle, with a host of banners flying. In front of the defending army there was a huge ogress riding a wolf, and the wolf was carrying a human carcass in its mouth, with blood streaming down its jaws; and as soon as the wolf had eaten the first corpse, she hurled another into its mouth, and then another and another, and the wolf gulped them all down. The ogress was chanting:

> *The ogress flaunts her crimson*
> *Shield as battle approaches;*
> *The troll-woman sees clearly*
> *The doom awaiting Harald.*
> *With greedy mouth she rends*
> *The flesh of fallen warriors;*
> *With frenzied hand she stains*
> *The wolf's jaws crimson –*
> *Wolf's jaws red with blood.*

82. King Harald's dream

ONE night King Harald himself dreamed that he was in Trondheim and met there his brother St Olaf; and Olaf spoke this stanza to him:

> *The warrior King Olaf*
> *Won many famous victories;*
> *I died a man of holiness*
> *Because I stayed in Norway.*

But now I fear, great Harald,
That death at last awaits you,
And wolves will rend your body;
God is not to blame.

Many other dreams and portents were reported at the time, and most of them were ominous.

Before King Harald left Trondheim he had had his son Magnus proclaimed king, and set him up as regent of Norway during his absence.

Thora Thorberg's-daughter also stayed behind; but Queen Elizabeth and their daughters Maria and Ingigerd went with Harald.

King Harald's son, Olaf, also went abroad with him.

83. Scarborough

WHEN King Harald was ready and the wind favourable he put out to sea; he himself made land in Shetland, but some of the fleet sailed direct to Orkney. Harald stayed in Shetland only briefly before sailing on to Orkney. There he gathered a large force. He was also joined by Earl Paul and Earl Erlend, the sons of Earl Thorfinn the Mighty; [1] but he left behind there Queen Elizabeth and their daughters, Maria and Ingigerd.

From Orkney he sailed south down the coast of Scotland and down the English coast, and landed at a place called Cleveland. He went ashore at once and started plundering, and subjugated the whole district; there was no resistance. King Harald

1. Earl Thorfinn the Mighty died about a year before Harald's invasion of England. The earldom of Orkney and Shetland was a separate Scandinavian realm, sometimes independent, sometimes subject to Norway; under Earl Thorfinn, during his fifty-year rule, it was extended to cover the Hebrides and the western and northern regions of the Scottish mainland. Erlend and Paul, Thorfinn's sons, ruled Orkney jointly for twenty years after Thorfinn's death.

then made for Scarborough and fought with the townsmen. He climbed up on to the rock that stands there, and had a huge pyre built on top of it and set alight; when the pyre was ablaze they used long pitchforks to hurl the burning faggots down into the town. One after another the houses caught fire, until the town was completely destroyed. The Norwegians killed a great number of people there and seized all the booty they could lay their hands on. The English then had no choice, if they wanted to stay alive, but to submit to King Harald. In this way he subdued the country wherever he went.

King Harald then proceeded south along the coast with all his army, and put in at Holderness, where he was met by some English troops. King Harald engaged them in battle, and defeated them.

84. Armies meet

AFTER that, King Harald went to the Humber, sailed up the river, and anchored his fleet close to the river bank.[1]

At that time, Earl Morcar and his brother Earl Waltheof were in York with a huge army.[2]

King Harald was lying at anchor in the Ouse when the earls' army came down to meet him; he went ashore and began to

1. According to English sources, King Harald landed at Riccall, on the left bank of the Ouse, three miles below the junction of the Ouse and the Wharfe, and ten miles south of York.

2. Earl Waltheof was not Earl Morcar's brother. The English chroniclers name Earl Morcar of Northumbria and his brother, Earl Edwin of Mercia (the sons of Earl Ælfgar) as the leaders of the English army at York (cf. page 131, note 1).

Earl Waltheof was the son of Earl Siward (Sigurd the Dane) of Northumbria; Siward ruled Northumbria from 1041 to 1055, and it was he who fought against Macbeth in 1054 and helped put Malcolm on the Scottish throne. Waltheof was too young to succeed to this turbulent earldom in 1055, and it was taken over by Earl Tostig; but King Edward the Confessor gave him an earldom in the Midlands.

draw up his army, with one flank reaching down to the river and the other stretching inland towards a dyke where there was a deep and wide swamp full of water.[1]

The English earls brought their army slowly down along the river in close formation. King Harald's standard was near the river, where his forces were thickest, but the thinnest and least reliable part of the line was at the dyke.

The earls now advanced down the line of the dyke, and the Norwegian flank there gave way; the English went after them, thinking that the Norwegians would flee. Earl Morcar's banner was in the van.

85. The Battle of Fulford

WHEN King Harald saw that the English flank was advancing down the dyke and was now opposite them, he sounded the attack and urged his men forward, with his banner, 'Land-Waster', carried in front. The Norwegian onslaught was so fierce that everything gave way before it, and a great number of the English were killed. The English army quickly broke into flight, some fleeing up the river, and others down the river; but most of them fled into the swamp, where the dead piled up so thickly that the Norwegians could cross the swamp dry-shod.

Earl Morcar lost his life there.[2] In the words of the poet Stein Herdisarson:

1. It is clear from English sources that King Harald advanced on York soon after landing at Riccall, and that the English army came out of York to bar his way to the city. The English drew up their army on the eastern bank of the Ouse near the village of Gate Fulford, two miles south of York.

2. The saga is mistaken here: Earl Morcar did not die at the Battle of Fulford. Both he and his brother, Earl Edwin, survived and made peace with the Norwegians, but their forces were too badly mauled to give Harold of England any support against the Norman invasion. The brothers later swore allegiance to William, but defected a few years later when the North rebelled against him.

Many were lost in the water;
The drowned sank to the bottom.
Warriors lay thickly fallen
Around the young Earl Morcar.
Harald's son, young Olaf,
Pursued the fleeing English
Running before King Harald.
Praise the brave prince Olaf.

This is from the poem which Stein Herdisarson composed in honour of King Harald's son, Olaf, and it makes it clear that Olaf took part in this battle with his father. This is also mentioned in the *Harald's Poem* :[1]

Waltheof's warriors
All lay fallen
In the swampy water,
Gashed by weapons;
And the hardy
Men of Norway
Could cross the marsh
On a causeway of corpses.

Earl Waltheof fled with the survivors towards the town of York, and there was great carnage there.

The battle was fought on the Wednesday before St Matthew's Day.[2]

86. At Stamford Bridge

EARL TOSTIG had travelled north from Flanders to join King Harald as soon as he arrived in England, and so the earl took part in all these battles.[3]

1. Nothing else is known about this poem, and no other fragment of it has survived.

2. 20 September 1066.

3. According to English sources, Earl Tostig came to England early in May and harried the Sussex coast before occupying Sandwich.

And just as Earl Tostig had told Harald previously, a large number of Englishmen came and joined them; these were Earl Tostig's friends and kinsmen, and they added greatly to the strength of Harald's army.

After the battle which has just been described, most of the people in the surrounding district submitted to King Harald, but some fled.

King Harald now prepared to advance on the town of York, and assembled his army at Stamford Bridge; [1] and since he had won such a great victory against powerful chieftains and a mighty army, all the inhabitants were too frightened to offer any resistance. So the townspeople decided to send a message to King Harald, offering to deliver themselves and the town into his power.

In accordance with this offer, King Harald marched on York with all his army on the Sunday.[2] Just outside the town he held an assembly of his men, attended also by representatives of the townspeople. All the townspeople gave their allegiance to King Harald, and gave him as hostages the sons of all the leading men; Earl Tostig knew about everyone in the town.

In the evening, King Harald went back to his ships, de-

His brother, King Harold of England, saw this as the forerunner of an invasion from Normandy; he mobilized the largest fleet and army England had ever known, and marched to Sandwich. Tostig retreated northwards, but when he attempted to land at the Humber he was driven off by Earl Edwin and Earl Morcar. He escaped with twelve small ships to Scotland, where he spent the summer raising forces with which to join King Harald of Norway in his invasion of England, as they had planned.

1. Stamford Bridge is on the River Derwent, seven miles east of York, although the saga author clearly thought it was close to the Norwegian naval headquarters at Riccall. This was where all the roads of eastern Yorkshire converged on the crossing of the Derwent, and was a strategic position from which to dominate the county while negotiating the capitulation of York. But it is a little hard to understand why King Harald should have camped with his army so far away from his ships.

2. 24 September 1066.

lighted with this easy victory; it had been agreed to hold a meeting in the town early the next morning, at which King Harald was to appoint officials to rule the town and distribute titles and estates.[1]

But that very same evening after sunset, King Harold Godwinsson of England arrived at York from the south with a huge army, and rode straight into the town with the full consent of all the townspeople. Then all the town's gates were closed and all the roads blocked, so that the news should not reach the Norwegians. The English army spent the night in the town.[2]

87. The armies meet

ON Monday, when King Harald Sigurdsson had breakfasted, he ordered the trumpets to sound the order for disembarkation. He got the army ready and divided his forces, choosing which of them were to go with him and which were to stay behind:

1. In fact, the meeting was to be held at Stamford Bridge, where hostages from the rest of Yorkshire were to be brought to King Harald. According to English sources, York capitulated on the day of the Battle of Fulford, but King Harald, instead of occupying the city, accepted provisions and hostages and then took his army back to his ships at Riccall. A treaty was arranged, whereby the citizens of York would join the Norwegians and march south with them to attempt the conquest of all England. Harald then marched to Stamford Bridge, leaving his ships at Riccall, and camped there on Sunday, 24 September, to await the hostages from the county.

2. King Harold Godwinsson had no knowledge of the Norwegian invasion until Harald of Norway landed at Riccall. He set off at once from London on a forced march northwards, gathering reinforcements on the way. According to English sources, he spent the night of 24 September at Tadcaster, nine miles south-west of York; it was not until the following morning, 25 September, that he marched through York, which the Norwegians had not garrisoned; after a march of seventeen miles, he could scarcely have reached Stamford Bridge before noon.

from each company two men were to go for every one that was left behind.

Earl Tostig prepared his troops for landing to go with King Harald; the men who were left behind to guard the ships were the king's son, Olaf, Earl Paul and Earl Erlend of Orkney, and Eystein Orri, the noblest of all the landed men and dearest to the king, to whom the king had promised his daughter Maria in marriage.[1]

The weather was exceptionally fine, with warm sunshine; so the troops left their armour behind and went ashore with only their shields, helmets, and spears, and girt with swords. A number of them also had bows and arrows. They were all feeling very carefree.

But as they approached the town they saw a large force riding to meet them. They could see the cloud of dust raised by the horses' hooves, and below it the gleam of handsome shields and white coats of mail. King Harald halted his troops and summoned Earl Tostig, and asked him what army this could be. Earl Tostig said he thought it was likely to be a hostile force, although it was also possible that these were some of his kinsmen seeking mercy and protection from the king in exchange for their faith and fealty. The king said they had better wait there and find out more about this army. They did so; and the closer the army came, the greater it grew, and their glittering weapons sparkled like a field of broken ice.[2]

88. Preparations

KING HARALD SIGURDSSON said, 'We must now think up a good and effective plan, for it is quite obvious that these are hostile troops; it must be the king himself.'

Earl Tostig replied, 'The first thing to do is to turn and head back to our ships as quickly as possible for the rest of our men

1. *Eystein Orri was the son of Thorberg Arnason.* He was the brother of King Harald's concubine, Thora.

2. There is no suggestion in the English sources that Harold had any cavalry with him at Stamford Bridge; but the Housecarls,

and weapons. Then we will be in a stronger position to face them, or else we could let our ships protect us, for then the cavalry could not get at us.'

'I have another plan,' said King Harald. 'We shall send three brave warriors on the fastest horses we have, and let them ride with all speed to inform our men – and they will come to our help at once. The English will have a very hard fight of it before we accept defeat.'

The earl told the king to decide in this as in everything else, and added that it was by no means his own wish to flee.

So King Harald ordered his banner, 'Land-Waster', to be raised; it was carried by a man called Fridrek.

89. Battle array

KING HARALD now drew up his army, and formed a long and rather thin line; the wings were bent back until they met, thus forming a wide circle of even depth all the way round, with shields overlapping in front and above. The king himself was inside the circle with his standard and his own retinue of hand-picked men.

Earl Tostig was also stationed inside the circle with his own company, and he had his own banner.

The army was formed up in this way because King Harald knew that cavalry always attacked in small detachments and then wheeled away at once. The king said that his own retinue and Earl Tostig's company would make sorties to wherever the need was greatest : 'Our archers are also to stay here with us. Those in the front rank are to set their spear-shafts into the ground and turn the points towards the riders' breasts when they charge us; and those immediately behind are to set their spears against the horses' chests.'

---

although they always fought on foot, were always mounted during marches. The saga account may be coloured here by stories of the *Norman* cavalry at Hastings.

90. Harold Godwinsson

KING HAROLD GODWINSSON had arrived there with a vast army, both cavalry and infantry.[1]

King Harald of Norway now rode round his lines to inspect the formation. He was riding a black horse with a blaze, which stumbled under him, and threw him off forwards. The king jumped quickly to his feet and said, 'A fall is fortune on the way.'

Then King Harold of England said to some Norwegians who were with him, 'Did you recognize that big man who fell off his horse, the man with the blue tunic and the beautiful helmet?'

'That was the king himself,' they said.

The king of England said, 'What a big, formidable-looking man he is: let us hope his good luck has now run out.'

91. 'Seven feet of ground'

TWENTY horsemen from the English king's company of House-carls came riding up to the Norwegian lines; they were all wearing coats of mail, and so were their horses.

One of the riders said, 'Is Earl Tostig here in this army?'

Tostig replied, 'There is no denying it – you can find him here.'

Another of the riders said, 'Your brother King Harold sends you his greetings, and this message to say you can have peace and the whole of Northumbria as well. Rather than have you refuse to join him, he is prepared to give you one third of all his kingdom.'

1. It is unlikely that Harold had more than 6,000 troops, all of them infantry. The 3,000-strong Royal Housecarls were reinforced by local militia called up en route for York – the so-called Select Fyrd; there were, in effect, Territorial reservists, bound by law to provide sixty days' service at a time.

The earl answered, 'This is very different from all the hostility and humiliation he offered me last winter. If this offer had been made then, many a man who is now dead would still be alive, and England would now be in better state. But if I accept this offer now, what will he offer King Harald Sigurdsson for all his effort?'

The rider said, 'King Harold has already declared how much of England he is prepared to grant him: seven feet of ground, or as much more as he is taller than other men.'

Earl Tostig said, 'Go now and tell King Harold to make ready for battle. The Norwegians will never be able to say that Earl Tostig abandoned King Harald Sigurdsson to join his enemies when he came west to fight in England. We are united in our aim: either to die with honour, or else conquer England.'

The horsemen now rode back.

Then King Harald Sigurdsson asked, 'Who was that man who spoke so well?'

'That was King Harold Godwinsson,' replied Tostig.

King Harald Sigurdsson said, 'I should have been told much sooner. These men came so close to our lines that this Harold should not have lived to tell of the deaths of our men.'

'It is quite true, sire,' said Earl Tostig, 'that the king acted unwarily, and what you say could well have happened. But I realized that he wanted to offer me my life and great dominions, and I would have been his murderer if I had revealed his identity. I would rather that he were my killer than I his.'

King Harald Sigurdsson said to his men, 'What a little man that was; but he stood proudly in his stirrups.'

It is said that King Harald Sigurdsson composed this stanza at the time:

> We go forward
> Into battle
> Without armour
> Against blue blades.
> Helmets glitter.
> My coat of mail
> And all our armour
> Are at the ships.

His coat of mail was called Emma; it was so long that it reached below his knee, and so strong that no weapon could pierce it. King Harald then said, 'That was a poor verse; I shall have to make a better one.' He composed another stanza:

> We never kneel in battle
> Before the storm of weapons
> And crouch behind our shields;
> So the noble lady told me.
> She told me once to carry
> My head always high in battle
> Where swords seek to shatter
> The skulls of doomed warriors.

Then the poet Thjodolf said:

> Though Harald himself should fall,
> Never shall I abandon
> The king's young heirs;
> God's will be done.
> The sun never shone
> On more promising princes;
> The two young eaglets
> Would soon avenge their father.

92. The Battle of Stamford Bridge

Now the battle began. The English made a cavalry charge on the Norwegians, who met it without flinching. It was no easy matter for the English to ride against the Norwegians because of their arrows, so they rode around them in a circle. There was only skirmishing to begin with, so long as the Norwegians kept their formation. The English cavalry kept charging them and falling back at once when they could make no headway.

The Norwegians observed this, and thought the enemy assaults rather half-hearted; so they launched an attack themselves on the retreating cavalry. But as soon as they had broken their shield-wall, the English rode down on them from all sides, showering spears and arrows on them.[1]

When King Harald Sigurdsson saw this, he led a charge into the thickest of the fighting. The battle became very fierce, and great numbers were killed on both sides. King Harald Sigurdsson now fell into such a fury of battle that he rushed forward ahead of his troops, fighting two-handed. Neither helmets nor coats of mail could withstand him, and everyone in his path gave way before him. It looked then as if the English were on the point of being routed. In the words of Arnor the Earls'-Poet:

> Norway's king had nothing
> To shield his breast in battle;
> And yet his war-seasoned
> Heart never wavered.
> Norway's warriors were watching
> The blood-dripping sword
> Of their courageous leader
> Cutting down his enemies.

But now King Harald Sigurdsson was struck in the throat by an arrow, and this was his death-wound. He fell, and with him fell all those who had advanced with him, except for those who retreated with the royal standard.

The battle still raged fiercely, and Earl Tostig was now fighting under the royal standard. Both sides drew back to form up again, and there was a long lull in the fighting. Then the poet Thjodolf said:

> Disaster has befallen us;
> I say the army has been duped.
> There was no cause for Harald
> To bring his forces westward.
> Mighty Harald is fallen
> And we are all imperilled;

1. This is another point where the saga account seems to echo the Battle of Hastings. It was the English at Hastings who broke formation to pursue the retreating Norman cavalry, only to be surrounded and cut down.

Norway's renowned leader
Has lost his life in England.

Before the fighting was resumed, Harold Godwinsson offered quarter to his brother Tostig and all the surviving Norwegians. But the Norwegians shouted back with one voice that every one of them would rather die than accept quarter from the English; they roared their war-cry, and the battle started again. In the words of Arnor the Earls'-Poet:

It was an evil moment
When Norway's king lay fallen;
Gold-inlaid weapons
Brought death to Norway's leader.
All King Harald's warriors
Preferred to die beside him,
Sharing their brave king's fate,
Rather than beg for mercy.

93. Orri's battle

AT this point Eystein Orri arrived from the ships with all the men he had; they were wearing coats of mail. Eystein took King Harald's banner, 'Land-Waster', and the fighting began for the third time, more fiercely than ever. The English fell in great numbers, and once again were on the point of being routed. This stage of the fighting was called Orri's Battle.

Eystein and his men had run all the way from the ships so hard that they were tired out and almost unable to fight before they arrived on the scene. But then they fell into such a battle fury that they did not bother to protect themselves as long as they could still stand on their feet. Eventually they threw off their coats of mail, and after that it was easy for the English to land blows on them; but some of the Norwegians collapsed from exhaustion and died unwounded. Nearly all the leading Norwegians were killed there.

It was now late in the afternoon. As was to be expected, not all reacted in the same way; a number of them fled, and others were lucky enough to survive in different ways. It had grown dark before the carnage ended.[1]

94. Styrkar's escape

KING HARALD SIGURDSSON'S marshal, Styrkar, an outstanding man, managed to escape. He got hold of a horse and rode away. In the evening a cold wind blew up, and since Styrkar was only wearing a shirt with a helmet on his head and a naked sword in his hand, as his weariness wore off he began to feel cold.

Then he met a cart-driver who was wearing a fur-lined leather coat.

'Would you like to sell your leather coat, my good man?' said Styrkar.

'Not to you,' he replied. 'You're a Norwegian, I can tell that from your speech.'

'And if I were a Norwegian, what would you do about it?'

'I'd try to kill you,' said the carter, 'but as luck would have it I don't have a weapon with me that would do.'

'Then since you can't kill me,' said Styrkar, 'I must see if I can't kill you.' And with that he raised his sword and swung

---

1. The saga account of the battle, although immensely vivid, conflicts with the *Anglo-Saxon Chronicle*, which is clearly more reliable. It seems that Harald of Norway never set out for York at all, but was surprised by the English army in his encampment on the east side of the Derwent. Taken unawares, the Norwegians failed to hold the wooden bridge over the river, despite an epic single-handed defence by an unnamed Norwegian giant who killed more than forty men with his battle-axe. When he was felled at last, the English army poured over the bridge and eventually overwhelmed the Norwegian army, one third of which was several miles away at Riccall, guarding the ships. All the sources agree that King Harald and Earl Tostig were killed, and that there was terrible slaughter on both sides.

it at the man's neck, slicing off his head. Then he took the leather coat, mounted his horse, and rode off down to the coast.

95. The Norman invasion

WILLIAM THE BASTARD, Duke of Normandy, heard that his kinsman King Edward had died, and also that Harold Godwinsson had been made king of England and crowned. William considered that he himself had a better right to the kingdom of England than Harold Godwinsson, since he was so closely related to King Edward.[1] William also felt he had a score to settle with Harold, who had insulted him by breaking the marriage deal with his daughter.[2]

Because of all this, William assembled an army in Normandy, a great number of men and plenty of ships.

On the day that he was riding from the town down to the ships, he had just mounted his horse when his wife came over to him and tried to talk to him. When he saw her, he kicked at her with his heel; his spur plunged deep into her breast, and she fell down dead at once.[3]

1. Duke William was the great-nephew of Queen Emma, King Edward's mother; William and Edward were second cousins. Duke William had no more claim to the throne than Harold, however, for England chose her kings by election at that time. The nearest male *heir* to the throne was Edgar the Ætheling, grandson of Edmund Ironside, who was still a child at the time. On the other hand, there are strong indications that King Edward the Confessor had once promised the throne to William – probably in 1051 or 1052, when William, it seems, may have visited the English court in person. King Edward often showed preference for Norman knights and churchmen during his reign; he had spent much of his twenty-five-year exile at the Norman court before succeeding to the throne of England, under the patronage of his cousin, Duke Robert, William's father.

2. All sources agree that William felt that Harold had broken his oath by taking the crown of England (cf. chapter 76).

3. There is an odd confusion here. Duchess Matilda lived, in fact,

The duke then rode off on his way to the ships.

He took his army over to England, and with him went his brother, Bishop Odo. As soon as the duke landed in England he started plundering, and subjugated the land wherever he went.[1]

William was exceptionally tall and strong, and a fine horseman. He was an oustanding warrior, but very cruel; he was very shrewd, but said not to be trustworthy.

96. The Battle of Hastings

KING HAROLD GODWINSSON gave King Harald's son, Olaf, leave to return home with the remnants of the Norwegian army that had survived the battle.[2]

Harold then turned south with his army, for he had heard that William the Bastard had landed in the south of England and was subjugating the country. With King Harold were his brothers Svein, Gyrth, and Waltheof.[3]

---

until November 1083. But William of Malmesbury relates a story that she was scourged to death with a bridle; and Norman sources tell of William's rough wooing of her – he beat her up severely, striking her with his fists, heels, and spurs.

1. The Norman army landed at Pevensey Bay on the morning of Thursday, 28 September, three days after the Battle of Stamford Bridge, and 250 miles to the south. It is thought that he had about 500 ships and an army of some 6,000 or 7,000 troops – including about 2,000 cavalry.

2. English sources relate that Harold did not attempt to destroy the routed remnants of the army which fled back to the ships at Riccall. He summoned Olaf and the two Orkney earls, Paul and Erlend, to his presence and allowed them to leave unharmed if they swore oaths that they would never again menace England. Only twenty-four ships, of that vast fleet of nearly 300 that had brought the invasion army to England, were required to take the survivors home – a measure of the terrible carnage of that battle.

3. Waltheof was not Harold's brother (cf. chapter 75), and Svein had died several years before this. Gyrth, Leofwin, and Wulfnoth were the three brothers who fought beside Harold at Hastings.

King Harold and Duke William met in the south of England at Hastings, where there was a fierce battle. King Harold was killed there; his brother Earl Gyrth and most of the English army also fell there. This was nineteen days after the death of King Harald Sigurdsson of Norway.[1]

Earl Waltheof managed to escape, and late in the evening he met a troop of William's men. When they saw the earl's men they fled into an oak-wood; there were about a hundred of them. Earl Waltheof had the wood set on fire, and they were all burned to death.[2] This is what the Poet Thorkel Skallason says in his *Waltheof's Poem* :[3]

> Waltheof burned a hundred
> Of William's Norman warriors
> As the fiery flames raged;
> What a burning there was that night!

1. 14 October 1066. The speed with which Harold hastened to deal with the Norman threat in the south is remarkable, and may well have contributed to his defeat. He can scarcely have heard the news of William's landing on 28 September before 1 October. He forced-marched his weary army 190 miles from York to London, gathering forces as he went; paused in London to assemble an army of some 6,000 or 7,000 men; and was at Hastings, in Sussex, fifty miles farther on, by the morning of Saturday, 14 October – only nineteen days after the Battle of Stamford Bridge. There is good reason to believe that his impatience to deal with William made him leave London with only half the size of army he could have mustered; and that his precipitate march through Sussex led him to clash unexpectedly with William on ground not of his own choosing.

2. It is not likely, according to other sources, that Earl Waltheof fought at Hastings. But this episode, and the stanza that commemorates it, may well refer to events in the north of England three years later, in 1069, when King Svein Ulfsson sent a Danish army to try to conquer England. Waltheof was one of the northern leaders who joined forces with the Danes; they attacked York, which was garrisoned by the Normans, and eventually took it by storm after the town had been fired. Waltheof was prominent in the slaughter that followed.

3. Thorkel Skallason was an Icelandic Court Poet in the retinue of Earl Waltheof.

William's sturdy warriors
Lay under the paws of wolves;
The grey beasts of carrion
Feasted on Norman flesh.

97. King William

WILLIAM had himself proclaimed King of England.[1] He sent a message to Earl Waltheof, offering a reconciliation, and promised him safe conduct to the meeting.

Earl Waltheof set out with only a few men; but when he reached the moor north of Castlebridge [2] he was met by two of King William's officers with a large force. They took him prisoner, and put him in shackles; later he was .beheaded. He is regarded as a saint by the English.[3] In the words of the poet Thorkel Skallason:

> *William crossed the cold Channel*
> *And reddened the bright swords,*
> *And now he has betrayed*
> *Noble Earl Waltheof.*
> *It's true that killing in England*
> *Will be a long time ending;*
> *A braver lord than Waltheof*
> *Will never be seen on earth.*

1. He was consecrated 'King of the English' in Westminster Abbey on 25 December 1066.

2. It is impossible to identify this place with any certainty. It could be Castleford, in Yorkshire.

3. After the Danish-inspired northern rebellion of 1069, Waltheof made his peace with King William. But in 1075, Waltheof once again joined a conspiracy of northern chieftains to overthrow King William. He withdrew from the plot at the last minute and threw himself on William's mercy; William forgave him, but never trusted him thereafter. Waltheof was tried for treason, and executed at Winchester on 31 May 1076. He was the only English leader executed by King William during his reign.

William was king of England for twenty-one years, and his descendants have been on the throne ever since.[1]

98. Back to Norway

OLAF HARALDSSON, the son of King Harald of Norway, took his army away from England. He set sail from Ravenspur, and reached Orkney in the autumn. There he heard the news that King Harald's daughter, Maria, had died suddenly on the very day and at the very hour that her father had been killed.

Olaf stayed in Orkney over the winter, and the following summer he sailed east to Norway, where he was proclaimed king jointly with his brother Magnus. Queen Elizabeth went to Norway with Olaf, her stepson, and so did her daughter Ingigerd.

A man called Skuli, who later came to be known as the king's foster-father, and his brother Ketil Hook also went to Norway with Olaf. The brothers were men of rank and came of a noble family in England; both of them were very shrewd men and very dear to King Olaf. Ketil Hook went north to Halogaland, where the king found him an excellent wife, and many important people are descended from him.

Skuli was an outstanding man, highly intelligent and extremely handsome. He became an officer of King Olaf's court and acted as his spokesman at public meetings and his adviser on all affairs of state.

King Olaf offered to give Skuli whatever province he wished to have, together with all the royal taxes and dues pertaining to it. Skuli thanked him for the offer, but said he would rather ask something else of him – 'For if there is a change of kings, that gift could be revoked,' he said. 'I would rather accept from you some estates that lie close to the market-towns where you, sire, are in the habit of celebrating Christmas.'

1. William died near Rouen on 9 September 1087.

The king agreed to this, and conferred on him several estates in the east near Konungahella, near Oslo, near Tonsberg, near Sarpsborg, near Bergen and in the north at Trondheim. All these were just about the finest estates in each district, and since then they have always belonged to Skuli's descendants.

King Olaf gave him in marriage his cousin Gudrun Nefstein's-daughter.[1] Their son was Asolf of Rein.[2]

99. Obituary on King Harald

A YEAR after King Harald Sigurdsson's death, his body was brought from England east to Norway. He was buried in the north at Trondheim, in St Mary's Church, which he himself had founded.

It was generally agreed that King Harald had surpassed all other men in shrewdness and resourcefulness, whether he was taking sudden decisions or making long-term plans for himself or others. He was an outstandingly brave warrior, and he also had great victory-luck, as has already been described. In the words of the poet Thjodolf:

> Denmark's noble enemy
> Always fought with courage;
> Harald showed by example
> That heart is half the victory.

King Harald was a handsome man of distinguished bearing. He was fair-haired, with a fair beard and long moustaches. One

1. Gudrun's mother was Ingirid, the daughter of Sigurd Sow and Asta; Ingirid was sister to King Harald Sigurdsson and half-sister to St Olaf.

2. Asolf married Thora, the daughter of Skopti Ogmundsson; their son was Guthorm of Rein, the father of Bard, the father of King Ingi and Duke Skuli.

Duke Skuli was regent in Norway during the minority of King Hakon Hakonsson (1204–63). He was host to Snorri Sturluson during his two visits to Norway in 1218 and 1236.

of his eyebrows was slightly higher than the other. He had long, well-shaped hands and feet. He was five ells tall.[1]

He was brutal to his enemies and dealt ruthlessly with any opposition to him. In the words of the poet Thjodolf:

> *Resourceful King Harald*
> *Punishes pride in his subjects;*
> *The king's guilty men*
> *Pay a heavy penalty.*
> *The punishment they get*
> *Is earned by their misdeeds;*
> *Each man gets his due deserts;*
> *Harald dispenses justice.*

King Harald was exceptionally greedy for power and valuable possessions. But he was very generous to those of his friends he liked. In the words of the poet Thjodolf:

> *Norway's liberal sea-king*
> *Gave me gold for my poetry;*
> *His royal favours are always*
> *Determined only by merit.*

King Harald was about fifty years old when he was killed.

We have no particular accounts about his youth until the age of fifteen, when he took part in the Battle of Stiklestad with his brother, King Olaf the Saint. After that he lived for another thirty-five years, and for all that time he was never free of unrest and war. King Harald never shirked a battle, but he often resorted to subterfuge when he had to deal with overwhelming odds. All who ever followed him in his battles and campaigns agree that in sudden peril he always took the course which everyone – afterwards – realized was the best.

1. The Icelandic ell was eighteen inches, which would make King Harald seven foot six inches tall – which is rather unlikely, even in the light of Harold Godwinsson's reference to 'seven feet of ground, or as much more as he is taller than other men' (cf. chapter 91). The 'ell' here may refer to an older, shorter Danish measure whose exact length is now unknown. But all accounts agree that King Harald was an exceptionally tall man.

100. A comparison

A MAN called Halldor, the son of Brynjolf Camel the Old, was a shrewd man and a great chieftain. This is what he said when he heard people saying how unlike one another the two brothers, St Olaf and King Harald, had been :

'I was held in high regard by both brothers, and so I knew their natures very well; and I have never known any two men so much alike. They were both highly intelligent and extremely brave in battle, hungry for wealth and power, imperious and haughty, able rulers, and ruthless in punishment. King Olaf forced the people to adopt Christianity and the true faith, and cruelly punished those who were slow to obey him. The chieftains would not endure his just and rightful rule and raised an army against him, and killed him in his own kingdom. For that reason he was made a saint.

'King Harald, however, went to war for fame and power, and he forced everyone he could into submission; and so he was killed in another king's land.

'Both brothers were considerate and generous in their everyday manner. They travelled widely, and were men of great enterprise. And all this made them outstanding and famous far and wide.'

101. King Magnus and King Olaf

KING MAGNUS HARALDSSON was the sole ruler of Norway for a year after King Harald's death, and then for two years he ruled the country jointly with his brother Olaf. Thus there were two kings in Norway; Magnus had the northern part of the kingdom, and Olaf the eastern part.

King Magnus had a son called Hakon; he was fostered by Thorir of Steig,[1] and was a most promising young man.

1. Thorir of Steig was King Harald Sigurdsson's cousin (cf. chapter 24).

After the death of King Harald Sigurdsson, King Svein Ulfsson of Denmark reckoned that the peace treaty between Norway and Denmark was no longer in force, since the treaty was only supposed to be valid as long as the two kings, Harald and Svein, were alive.

So once again, armies were levied in both kingdoms. Harald's sons raised a full levy of men and ships in Norway, and King Svein sailed north with a Danish army.

Then messengers went between them to try to preserve peace. The Norwegians said they would only accept the terms of the previous treaty, otherwise they would fight. That is why this stanza was composed:

> *Olaf guarded his kingdom*
> *With threats and offers of peace;*
> *And no king had the courage*
> *To try to take it from him.*

In the words of the poet Stein Herdisarson in *Olaf's Poem*:

> *The warrior king from Trondheim,*
> *Where his sainted uncle lies,*
> *Bravely defends his heritage*
> *Against the greed of Denmark.*
> *St Olaf gladly granted*
> *Norway to his descendants;*
> *No son of Svein of Denmark*
> *Has any right to claim it.*

At this meeting a treaty was made between the kings, and peace was assured for the two countries.

King Magnus became ill with ergotism, and lay sick in bed for some time. He died in Trondheim, and was buried there. He had been a popular king, well-liked by all the people.[1]

---

1. King Magnus Haraldsson died in 1069. His brother Olaf was sole king of Norway thereafter until 1093. After the turbulence of Harald Sigurdsson's reign, Norway now enjoyed a long period of peace, and Olaf came to be known as Olaf the Quiet.

Genealogical Tables

KING HARALD SIGURDSSON

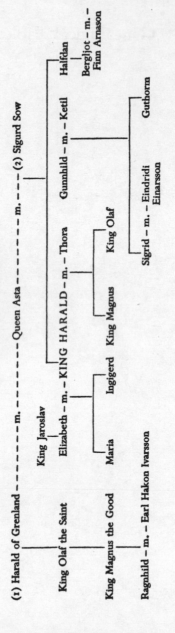

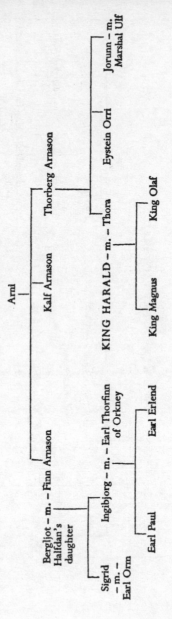

THE ARNASON FAMILY

Arni

Bergljot – m. – Finn Arnason   Kalf Arnason   Thorberg Arnason
Halfdan's
daughter

Sigrid   Ingibjorg – m. – Earl Thorfinn   KING HARALD – m. – Thora   Eystein Orri   Jorunn – m.
– m. –   of Orkney   Marshal Ulf
Earl Orm

Earl Paul   Earl Erlend   King Magnus   King Olaf

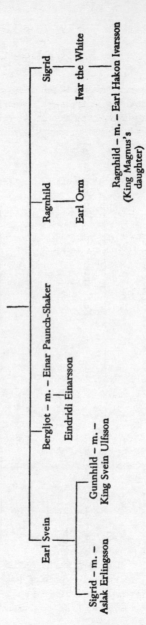

EARL HAKON THE POWERFUL

Earl Svein

Sigrid – m. –
Aslak Erlingsson

Gunnhild – m. –
King Svein Ulfsson

Bergljot – m. – Einar Paunch-Shaker

Eindridi Einarsson

Ragnhild

Earl Orm

Sigrid

Ivar the White

Ragnhild – m. – Earl Hakon Ivarsson
(King Magnus's
daughter)

Glossary of Proper Names

THIS Glossary of proper names is not a complete index to all the personal names that occur in the saga. Primarily it is intended as a guide to the relationships of the people who play a significant part in the saga, and an indexed summary of the part they play. The numbers refer to chapters, not pages.

ÆTHELRED THE UNREADY, King of England 979–1016 : father of King Edward the Confessor, 75.

ARNOR THORDARSON ('The Earls'-Poet'), Court Poet to the Norse Earls of Orkney : his poetry quoted, 52, 63, 92.

ASMUND (BJARNARSON), King Svein Ulfsson's nephew and foster-son : killed by Earl Hakon Ivarsson, 49.

ASTA GUDBRAND'S-DAUGHTER, mother of King Harald Sigurdsson and St Olaf, 1 (note 1, page 45): mother of Ingi-rid, 98.

ASTRID (SVEIN'S-DAUGHTER), daughter of King Svein Fork-Beard and mother of King Svein Ulfsson, 18 (note 2, page 65): half-sister to King Olaf Eiriksson of Sweden, and sister of King Knut (Canute) the Great.

BERGLJOT HAKON'S-DAUGHTER, daughter of Earl Hakon the Powerful, married to Einar Paunch-Shaker, 40: mother of Eind-ridi Einarsson, 40; demands vengeance for the murder of Einar and Eindridi, 44; sends emissaries to Earl Hakon Ivarsson, 46.

BERGLJOT HALFDAN'S-DAUGHTER, niece of King Harald Sigurdsson : married to Finn Arnason, 45.

BOLVERK ARNORSSON, brother of Thjodolf Arnorsson, and Court Poet to King Harald Sigurdsson : his poetry quoted, 2, 24, 32.

CANUTE THE GREAT. See Knut Sveinsson.

CONSTANTINE MONOMACHUS, emperor of Byzantium 1042–55: husband of Empress Zoe, 13; blinded by Harald Sigurdsson in Constantinople, 14.

DOTTA, daughter of a Danish farmer, Thorkel Geysa : mocks King Harald Sigurdsson of Norway, 32.

EACHMARGACH, king in Ireland. See Margad.

EDITH, Queen of England : daughter of Earl Godwin of Wessex, married to King Edward the Confessor, 75.

EDWARD THE CONFESSOR, King of England 1042–66: married

to Queen Edith, daughter of Earl Godwin of Wessex, 75; death and burial in London, 77; popularity in England, 79; news of his death reaches William of Normandy, 95.

EINAR PAUNCH-SHAKER, chieftain in the north of Norway: refuses to invade Denmark with King Harald Sigurdsson after King Magnus the Good's death, 29; takes Magnus's body to Trondheim, 30; father of Eindridi Einarsson, 40; enmity with King Harald, 43; rescues a prisoner from the king's court, is murdered with his son by King Harald, 44.

EINDRIDI EINARSSON, son of Einar Paunch-Shaker: married to Sigrid Ketil's-daughter, niece of King Harald Sigurdsson, 40; murdered with his father by King Harald, 44; consequences of his murder, 45-7.

ELIZABETH (ELLISIF), daughter of King Jaroslav of Novgorod: King Harald Sigurdsson alludes to her in a love poem, 15; marries King Harald, 17; granddaughter of King Olaf Eiriksson of Sweden, 18; has two daughters by King Harald – Maria and Ingigerd, 33; accompanies King Harald west to Britain in 1066, 82; stays in Orkney, 83; returns to Norway with her stepson, Olaf, after King Harald's death, 98.

EMMA, Queen of England; wife of King Æthelred the Unready and King Knut Sveinsson, mother of King Edward the Confessor, and daughter of Richard I, Duke of Normandy, 75.

ERLEND THORFINNSSON, joint Earl of Orkney with his brother Paul: son of Earl Thorfinn the Mighty, joins King Harald's invasion of England, 83; guards the Norwegian ships at Riccall, thus escaping the slaughter at Stamford Bridge, 87.

EYSTEIN ERLENDSSON, Archbishop at Trondheim 1161-88: descendant of Ulf Ospaksson, 9 (note 2, page 55), 37 (note 2, page 88); founds Nidaros Cathedral in Trondheim, 38.

EYSTEIN ORRI, Norwegian nobleman and prospective son-in-law to King Harald Sigurdsson: son of Thorberg Arnason and brother of King Harald's concubine, 87; guards the Norwegian ships at Riccall, 87; leads the Norwegian reinforcements to King Harald's aid at Stamford Bridge, fights 'Orri's Battle', 93.

FINN ARNASON, chieftain in the north of Norway: married to King Harald Sigurdsson's niece, Bergljot Halfdan's-daughter, and uncle of King Harald's concubine, 45; sent by King Harald to mediate with Hakon Ivarsson after the murder of Einar Paunch-Shaker, 45-7; arranges a reconciliation between his brother, Kalf Arnason, and King Harald, 51; blames King Harald for Kalf's death, goes to Denmark, becomes Earl of Halland there, 53;

fights beside King Svein Ulfsson of Denmark against King Harald at the Battle of the Nissa, 62; captured by King Harald, 63; insults King Harald, is released by him, 66.

GEORGIOS MANIAKES, leader of the Byzantine army, 3; disputes precedence at camping-sites with Harald Sigurdsson, loses, 4; divides the army, returns to Constantinople, 5, 11 note 1, page 58).

GODWIN WULFNOTHSSON, Earl of Wessex: father of Harold Godwinsson and Tostig, father-in-law of King Edward the Confessor, 75.

GRANI, an Icelandic Court Poet: his verse quoted, 32.

GUNNHILD SIGURD'S-DAUGHTER, daughter of Sigurd Sow and sister of King Harald Sigurdsson: mother-in-law of Eindridi Einarsson, 40 (note 1, page 90); mother of Guthorm Gunnhildarson, 45 (note 3, page 94), 53.

GUNNHILD SVEIN'S-DAUGHTER, granddaughter of Earl Hakon the Powerful: married to King Svein Ulfsson of Denmark, 41.

GUTHORM GUNNHILDARSON, nephew of King Harald Sigurdsson: out on Viking raids with Finn Arnason and Hakon Ivarsson, 45; close friend to King Harald Sigurdsson, 54; in league with King Margad of Ireland, is challenged by him to fight, wins battle in the Menai Strait, donates silver crucifix to St Olaf's Church in Trondheim, 54-5.

GYDA (THORGILS'-DAUGHTER), wife of Earl Godwin of Wessex: aunt of King Svein Ulfsson of Denmark, 75 (note 3, page 130); mother of Earl Tostig, 78.

GYRTH GODWINSSON, son of Earl Godwin of Wessex: brother of Harold Godwinsson, 75 (note 1, page 131); killed at the Battle of Hastings, 96.

HAKON IVARSSON, chieftain of the Uplands, in Norway: his outstanding qualities, great-grandson of Earl Hakon the Powerful, 39; inherits feud after the murder of Einar Paunch-Shaker and Eindridi, 44-6; agrees with Finn Arnason to drop the feud if he can mary Ragnhild, daughter of King Magnus the Good, 47; woos Ragnhild, is rejected, asks King Harald Sigurdsson for an earldom, is refused, leaves Norway and joins King Svein Ulfsson of Denmark as commander of Denmark's land-defences, 48; kills King Svein's kinsman, Asmund, and leaves King Svein's service, 49; reconciliation with King Harald, marries Ragnhild, becomes an earl, 50; fights beside King Harald at the Battle of the Nissa, 61-3; saves King Svein Ulfsson's life, smuggles him ashore, 64; is praised for his part in the battle, 68; hears of a threatened attack by King Harald, escapes to Sweden, 69; becomes Earl of Varmland in Sweden, collects his usual dues from the Uplands, 70; fights King Harald in Gotaland, loses, but escapes, 72.

HAKON SIGURDSSON (Earl Hakon the Powerful), ruler of Norway 975–95: great-grandfather of Hakon Ivarsson, 39; father-in-law of Einar Paunch-Shaker, 40; grandfather of King Svein Ulfsson's wife, 41.

HALL KODRAN'S-KILLER (OTRYGGSSON): killed by Thormod Eindridason in vengeance for Kodran, 72.

HALLDOR BRYNJOLFSSON, a Norwegian chieftain: compares King Harald Sigurdsson and St Olaf, 100.

HALLDOR SNORRASON, an Icelander in the Varangian Guard: son of Snorri the Priest, and ancestor of Snorri Sturluson, 9; companion of Harald Sigurdsson in the Mediterranean, accuses him of timidity in battle, 9; imprisoned with Harald in Constantinople, escapes with him, 14; returns to Norway with Harald, then goes back to Iceland, 36.

HARALD SIGURDSSON (HARALD HARDRADI), King of Norway: escapes from the Battle of Stiklestad, 1; goes to Russia and then Constantinople, 2; becomes leader of the Varangian Guard, 3; disputes with the commander-in-chief of the Byzantine army, 4; campaigns in the Land of the Saracens, 5; campaigns in Sicily, 6–10; returns to Constantinople, 11; campaigns in Palestine, 12; imprisoned in Constantinople, 13; escapes and blinds the emperor, 14; escapes to Novgorod and claims all the treasure he had been amassing there, 15–16; marries Elizabeth, daughter of King Jaroslav, 17; goes to Sweden and makes alliance with Svein Ulfsson of Denmark, 18; campaigns in Denmark with Svein, 19; his nephew, King Magnus the Good of Norway, offers terms, 20–1; breaks with Svein Ulfsson and meets Magnus, 22; shares wealth in return for joint share of the throne of Norway, 23–4; disputes with Magnus, 27; plans invasion of Denmark with Magnus, 27–8; claims crown of Denmark as well as Norway after Magnus's death, returns to Norway, 29; expedition to Denmark against King Svein Ulfsson, 32; 'marries' a concubine, Thora, and has two sons by her, 33; expedition to Denmark, burns Hedeby, escapes with difficulty, 34–5; relations with Iceland, 36–7; church-building in Trondheim, 38; growing imperiousness, 42; murders Einar Paunch-Shaker and his son, 43–4; sends Finn Arnason to mediate with Hakon Ivarsson, 45; breaks agreement with Hakon Ivarsson, 48; reconciliation with Hakon, 50; reconciliation with Kalf Arnason, arranges his death, 51–2; another expedition to

Denmark, escapes with difficulty, 58; builds a huge warship, 59; challenges King Svein to a decisive battle, 59–60; fights King Svein at the Battle of the Nissa, wins, 61–3; teases Finn Arnason, releases him, 66; grows jealous of Hakon Ivarsson's prowess, 68; tries to attack Hakon Ivarsson in the Uplands, 69; peace treaty with Denmark, 71; defeats Hakon Ivarsson in battle, 72; punitive expeditions within Norway, 73; plans invasion of England with Earl Tostig, 79; gathers forces for the invasion, hears portents, 80–2; sails to Orkney, harries east coast of England, 83; lands in Yorkshire, defeats an English army before York at the Battle of Fulford, 84–5; moves Norwegian army to Stamford Bridge, 86; meets King Harold of England in battle, 87–92; killed at the Battle of Stamford Bridge, 92; his body taken to Trondheim, 99; obituary, 99; Harald compared with his half-brother, St Olaf, 100.

HARDA-KNUT, King of England 1040–2 : succeeded by Edward the Confessor, 75; agreement with King Magnus the Good of Norway that each would inherit the other's kingdoms, 79.

HAROLD GODWINSSON, Earl of Wessex and King of England : son of Earl Godwin, and a favourite of King Edward the Confessor, 75; stays with William of Normandy, is betrothed to his daughter, 76; elected and crowned king of England after Edward the Confessor's death, 77; outlaws his brother, Earl Tostig, 78; marches to York to face King Harald Sigurdsson's invasion, 86; meets Harald of Norway in the Battle of Stamford Bridge, wins victory, 87–92; allows King Harald's son, Olaf, to return to Norway with the remnants of the Norwegian army, 96; defeated by William of Normandy at the Battle of Hastings, 96.

ILLUGI THE BRYNJUDALE-POET, an Icelandic Court Poet : his poetry quoted, 5.

INGIGERD HARALD'S-DAUGHTER, daughter of King Harald Sigurdsson : born, 33; sails with King Harald, stays in Orkney with her mother, Queen Elizabeth, 82–3; returns to Norway, 98.

INGIRID SIGURD'S-DAUGHTER, daughter of Sigurd Sow and sister of King Harald Sigurdsson : mother of Gudrun, who marries Skuli, 98.

IVAR THE WHITE, grandson of Earl Hakon the Powerful : father of Hakon Ivarsson, 39.

JAROSLAV, ruler of Russia 1036–54 : welcomes Harald Sigurdsson to his court in Novgorod, 2; looks after treasure Harald Sigurdsson sends from his Mediterranean campaigns, 5; welcomes Harald back to Novgorod, gives him his daughter Elizabeth in marriage, 16–17.

KALF ARNASON, brother of Finn Arnason: in exile from Norway, 45; returns for a reconciliation with King Harald Sigurdsson, 51; sent to his death in battle by King Harald, 52.

KARL, a farmer in Halland: shelters the disguised King Svein Ulfsson after the Battle of the Nissa, 64; rewarded by King Svein, 67.

KETIL HOOK, a nobleman in England: goes to Norway with King Olaf Haraldsson, settles there, 98.

KETIL KALF, married to Gunnhild, King Harald Sigurdsson's sister: father of Sigrid, wife of Eindridi Einarsson, 40; father of Guthorm Gunnhildarson, 54.

KNUT SVEINSSON (Canute the Great), King of Denmark, Norway, and England, 13 (note 1, page 60); uncle of King Svein Ulfsson of Denmark, 18 (notes 1 and 2, page 65); father of King Harda-Knut of England, 75 (note 1, page 130); his conquests, 78.

MAGNUS HARALDSSON, joint king of Norway 1066-9: son of King Harald Sigurdsson and his concubine Thora, 33; with King Harald at the Battle of the Nissa, 66; saves Thormod Eindridason after the killing of Hall Kodran's-Killer, 72; said to have attempted the conquest of England in 1058, 79 (note 1, page 137); stays in Norway as regent for King Harald during the invasion of Britain in 1066, 82; joint king of Norway with his brother Olaf, 98; dies, 101.

MAGNUS OLAFSSON (MAGNUS THE GOOD), King of Norway and Denmark 1035-47: son of St Olaf, nephew of King Harald Sigurdsson, succeeds to the throne, 13; defeats Svein Ulfsson at the Battle of Helganess, 18; hears that Harald Sigurdsson is invading Denmark in alliance with Svein Ulfsson, 20; sends conciliatory messages to Harald Sigurdsson, 21; meets Harald, gives him a half-share in the crown of Norway in return for half his wealth, 22-4; joint king of Norway with Harald, 25; disputes with King Harald, 27; expedition to Denmark with Harald, dies there, bequeaths Denmark to Svein Ulfsson, 28; his followers, 29; his body taken to Trondheim, 30; obituary, 30; King Svein inherits Denmark from him, 31; King Harald inherits all Norway from him, 32; builder of St Olaf's Church in Trondheim, 38; his daughter Ragnhild wooed by Hakon Ivarsson, 47, 48, 50; his banner carried by Earl Hakon Ivarsson, 72; chronology, 74; his claim to the throne of England, 78 (note 1, page 136), 79.

MARGAD ROGNVALDSSON (EACHMARGACH), King in Dublin: in league with Guthorm Gunnhildarson, 54; tries to deprive Guthorm of booty, is killed by him in battle, 55.

MARIA, daughter of Empress Zoe of Constantinople: wooed by Harald Sigurdsson, 13; abducted by Harald, then sent back to Constantinople, 15.

MARIA HARALD'S-DAUGHTER, daugher of King Harald Sigurdsson and Queen Elizabeth, 33; accompanies King Harald to Britain, 82; stays in Orkney with her mother, 83; betrothed to Eystein Orri, 87; dies at the moment of her father's death, 98.

[MATILDA, wife of William of Normandy: befriends Harold of England, 76; killed by William, 95.]

MICHAEL CATALACTUS (MICHAEL IV), Byzantine Emperor 1034–41; Harald Sigurdsson comes to his court, 3; mentioned in a poem, 5; his reign, 11 (notes 1 and 2, page 58).

MICHAEL CALAPHATES (MICHAEL V), Byzantine Emperor 1041–2; succeeds Michael IV, 13 (note 1, page 61); blinded, 14 (note 1, page 62).

MORCAR, Earl of Northumbria: said to be son of Earl Godwin, 75; leads the English army against King Harald Sigurdsson at the Battle of Fulford and is defeated, 84; said to have died in the battle, 85.

ODD THE KIKINA-POET, an Icelandic Court Poet: his poetry quoted, 28.

OLAF EIRIKSSON, King of Sweden: grandfather of King Harald Sigurdsson's wife, Elizabeth, and uncle of King Svein Ulfsson, 18.

OLAF HARALDSSON (ST OLAF), King of Norway 1016–30: killed at the Battle of Stiklestad, 1; father of King Magnus the Good, 13; appears to Harald Sigurdsson in a vision, rescues him from prison, 14; owner of a bracelet he gave to King Magnus, 24; his shrine looked after by King Magnus, 25; comes to King Magnus in a deathbed dream, 28; his shrine in St Clement's Church, Trondheim, 30; sent timber for a church in Iceland, 36; his church built in Trondheim, 38; the uprising against him, 46; only allowed one earl in the kingdom, 48; miracles reported – at Guthorm's battle with Margad, 55; in Denmark, 56, in London, 57; his shrine locked by King Harald before leaving for Britain, 80; brother of Ingirid, 98; St Olaf and King Harald compared, 100.

OLAF HARALDSSON (OLAF THE QUIET), King of Norway 1067–93: son of King Harald Sigurdsson and his concubine Thora, 33; goes to Britain with King Harald, 82–3; fights at the Battle of Fulford with King Harald, 85; guards the Norwegian ships at Riccall and thus escapes the slaughter at Stamford Bridge, 87; is allowed by Harold of England to take the Norwegian survivors home, 96; goes first to Orkney, then Norway, becomes joint king with his brother Magnus Haraldsson, 98; his reign, 101.

ORM (EILIFSSON), Earl of the Uplands: grandson of Earl Hakon the Powerful, 41; son-in-law of Finn Arnason, 46; his earldom confirmed by King Harald, 48; dies, 50.

ODO, Bishop of Bayeux, brother of William of Normandy: accompanies William on the invasion of Britain, 95.

PAUL THORFINNSSON, joint Earl of Orkney: son of Earl Thorfinn the Mighty, joins King Harald Sigurdsson in his invasion of England, 83; guards the Norwegian ships at Riccall, thus escaping the slaughter at Stamford Bridge, 87.

RAGNHILD HAKON'S-DAUGHTER, daughter of Earl Hakon the Powerful: mother of Earl Orm of the Uplands, 41 (note 2, page 90).

RAGNHILD MAGNUS'S-DAUGHTER, daughter of King Magnus the Good: promised to Hakon Ivarsson by Finn Arnason, 47; wooed by Hakon Ivarsson, refuses him, 48; marries Hakon Ivarsson, 50.

RICHARD, DUKE OF NORMANDY (Richard the Fearless): father of Queen Emma of England, 75.

ROBERT, DUKE OF NORMANDY (Robert the Magnificent): said to be brother of Queen Emma of England (actually her nephew), 75; father of William of Normandy, 75.

ROGNVALD BRUSASON, Earl of Orkney: helps Harald Sigurdsson escape from the Battle of Stiklestad, 1.

SIGRID FINN'S-DAUGHTER, daughter of Finn Arnason: married to Earl Orm of the Uplands, 46.

SIGRID KETIL'S-DAUGHTER, daughter of Gunnhild Sigurd's-daughter and kinswoman of King Harald Sigurdsson: married to Eindridi Einarsson, 40.

SIGRID SVEIN'S-DAUGHTER, granddaughter of Earl Hakon the Powerful: married to Aslak Erlingsson, 41.

SIGURD SOW (HALFDANARSON), provincial king of Ringerike in Norway: father of King Harald Sigurdsson, 1; father of Gunnhild, 40; grandfather of Bergljot, the wife of Finn Arnason, 45; grandfather of Guthorm Gunnhildarson, 45 (note 2, page 94); father of Ingirid, 98.

SKULI, nobleman in England: foster-father to King Olaf the Quiet, goes to Norway with him, marries Gudrun Nefstein's-daughter, King Olaf's cousin, 98.

SKULI BARDARSON (DUKE SKULI), d. 1240, regent of Norway for King Hakon Hakonsson: descendant of Skuli, King Olaf the Quiet's foster-father, 98 (note 2, page 160).

SNORRI THE PRIEST, father of Halldor Snorrason, 9.

STEIN HERDISARSON, an Icelandic Court Poet: author of 'Ulf's Poem', 37; his poetry quoted, 61; takes part in the Battle of the Nissa on Marshal Ulf's ship, 61; his poetry quoted, 62, 63, 85, 101.

STEINKEL, King of Sweden: welcomes Hakon Ivarsson, puts him in charge of Varmland, 69–70; gives Hakon Ivarsson troops to fight King Harald Sigurdsson, 72.

STUF THORDARSON (STUF THE BLIND), an Icelandic Court Poet: his poetry quoted, 12, 17, 33, 34.

STYRKAR, King Harald Sigurdsson's marshal: escapes from the Battle of Stamford Bridge, 94.

SVEIN GODWINSSON, son of Earl Godwin of Wessex, 75; said to have fought at the Battle of Hastings, 96.

SVEIN ULFSSON, King of Denmark 1047–74: claims throne of Denmark, is defeated by King Magnus the Good at the Battle of Helganess, 18; meets Harald Sigurdsson, makes alliance with him, invades Denmark, 18–19; parts with Harald Sigurdsson, 22; takes refuge off Skaane when King Magnus and King Harald invade Denmark, 26; flees to Skaane again, 28; inherits Denmark from King Magnus, 28, 31; challenges King Harald to battle at the Gota River, doesn't turn up, attacks Harald later, almost catches him, 34–5; married to Gunnhild Svein's-daughter, 41; welcomes Hakon Ivarsson, 48; dismisses Hakon Ivarsson after his kinsman Asmund is killed, 49; makes Finn Arnason Earl of Halland, 53; nearly catches King Harald again, 58; challenges Harald, loses the Battle of the Nissa, 59–63; escapes with Hakon Ivarsson's help, 64; rewards Karl for his help, 67; peace treaty with King Harald, 71; refuses to help his kinsman Earl Tostig invade England, 78; attacks Norway after King Harald's death, makes peace with King Harald's sons, 101.

THJODOLF ARNARSSON, an Icelandic Court Poet: his poetry quoted, 1, 2, 5, 11, 14, 18, 20, 22, 32, 42, 60, 61, 63, 72, 73, 74, 91, 92, 99.

THORA THORBERG'S-DAUGHTER, King Harald Sigurdsson's concubine: 'marries' King Harald, has two sons by him – Magnus and Olaf, 33; sister of Jorunn, Marshal Ulf's wife, 37; niece of Finn Arnason, 45; with King Harald after the Battle of the Nissa, 66; stays behind in Norway when King Harald invades England, 83.

THORARIN SKEGGJASON, an Icelandic Court Poet: his poetry quoted, 14.

THORBERG ARNASON, brother of Finn Arnason, and father of

King Harald Sigurdsson's concubine, Thora, 33; father of Jorunn, Marshal Ulf's wife, 37; father of Eystein Orri, 87.

THORFINN SIGURDSSON (THORFINN THE MIGHTY), Earl of Orkney 1014–65 : entertains Kalf Arnason, 51; his sons Paul and Erlend join King Harald Sigurdsson on his invasion of England, 83.

THORIR, half-brother to King Magnus the Good : sent by King Magnus to Svein Ulfsson, to bequeath Denmark to Svein, 28; comes to Denmark, is welcomed by Svein, 31.

THORIR OF STEIG (THORDARSON), cousin to King Harald Sigurdsson : confers crown of Norway on King Harald, is given gifts by him, 24; foster-father to Hakon, son of King Magnus Haraldsson, 101.

THORKEL SKALLASON, an Icelandic Court Poet : his poetry quoted, 96.

THORLEIK THE HANDSOME, an Icelandic Court Poet : goes to Denmark to compose a eulogy in honour of King Svein Ulfsson, 34; his poetry quoted, 34, 35.

THORMOD EINDRIDASON, kills Hall Kodran's-Killer, escapes, 72.

TOSTIG GODWINSSON, Earl of Northumbria, brother of Harold of England : son of Earl Godwin of Wessex, 75; said to be commander-in-chief of the English armed forces, 77; objects to Harold being elected king of England, 77; goes into exile in Flanders, appeals to his kinsman King Svein Ulfsson of Denmark for help in invading England, is refused, 78; appeals for help to King Harald Sigurdsson of Norway, accepted, 79; sails to Flanders to raise troops, 79; joins King Harald's invasion, collects supporters in the north of England, 86; helps King Harald win Battle of Fulford, 86; with King Harald at the Battle of Stamford Bridge, 87; refuses his brother Harold's offer of a truce and half of England, 91; fights under King Harald's banner after Harald's death, refuses another truce offer from his brother Harold, 92.

ULF OSPAKSSON (MARSHAL ULF), Icelander in King Harald Sigurdsson's service : in Harald's company of Varangians, 9; imprisoned with Harald in Constantinople, escapes with him, 14; goes to Norway with Harald, 36; becomes King Harald's marshal, marries Jorunn, the sister of King Harald's concubine, 37; fights in the Battle of the Nissa, 61; dies, mourned by King Harald, 79.

ULF THORGILSSON (EARL ULF), father of King Svein Ulfsson : his history, 18 (note 1, page 65); brother of Gyda, Earl Tostig's mother, 78.

VALGARD OF VOLL, an Icelandic Court Poet : his poetry quoted, 17, 19.

Chronological Table, 1030–66

(Numbers in brackets refer to chapters of the saga)

Battle of Stiklestad in Norway (1)	31 Aug. 1030
Svein Knutsson becomes ruler of Norway (13)	1030
Harald Sigurdsson goes to Russia (2)	1031
King Magnus the Good becomes ruler of Norway (13)	1035
Duke William, aged seven, succeeds to Normandy (75)	1035
Knut Sveinsson (Canute the Great) dies (13)	1035
King Harda-Knut rules Denmark	1035–42
Harold Knutsson (King Harold I) rules England	1035–40
Harald Sigurdsson in Constantinople (3–15)	c. 1035–44
Varangian campaigns in Sicily (6–11)	1038–41
King Harda-Knut rules England	1040–42
Edward the Confessor rules England (75–7)	1042–66
King Magnus the Good inherits crown of Denmark (13)	1042
Harald Sigurdsson leaves Constantinople (15–17)	1044
King Magnus defeats Svein Ulfsson at Helganess (18)	1045
Harald Sigurdsson arrives in Sweden (17)	1045
Harald Sigurdsson becomes joint ruler of Norway (23–4)	1046
King Magnus the Good dies (28)	25 Oct. 1047
King Harald Sigurdsson sole ruler of Norway (32)	1047–66
King Svein Ulfsson rules Denmark (31)	1047–74
King Harald raids Denmark (32)	1048
King Harald burns Hedeby (34–5)	1049
Earl Godwin and his family exiled	1051
William of Normandy visits England(?)	1051 (?)
Guthorm Gunnhildarson kills King Margad (55)	28 July 1052
Earl Godwin dies	15 Apr. 1953
Tostig appointed Earl of Northumbria	1055
King Harald sends famine relief to Iceland (36)	1056
Battle of the Nissa (62–3)	9 Aug. 1062
Peace treaty between Norway and Denmark (71)	1064

Earl Harold visits Normandy (71)	c. 1064
Punitive measures against the Uplanders (73)	1065
Earl Tostig exiled to Flanders (78)	1065
Morcar becomes Earl of Northumbria	1065
Edward the Confessor dies (77)	5 Jan. 1066
Earl Harold Godwinsson crowned King of England	6 Jan. 1066
King Harald of Norway sails for England	Autumn 1066
Battle of Fulford (84–5)	20 Sep. 1066
Harald of Norway killed at Stamford Bridge (92)	25 Sep. 1066
William of Normandy lands at Pevensey (95)	28 Sep. 1066
Battle of Hastings (96)	14 Oct. 1066
William of Normandy crowned King of England (97)	25 Dec. 1066

Maps

ICELAND

Atlantic
Ocean

Trondheim

FAROES

FINLAND

SHETLAND

NORWAY

Bergen   Oslo

SWEDEN

ORKNEY

SCOTLAND

North Sea

Baltic Sea

DENMARK

Dublin

York

IRELAND

London

NORMANDY

FLANDERS

Rouen

Paris

ITALY

SICILY

AFRICA

Mediterranean Sea

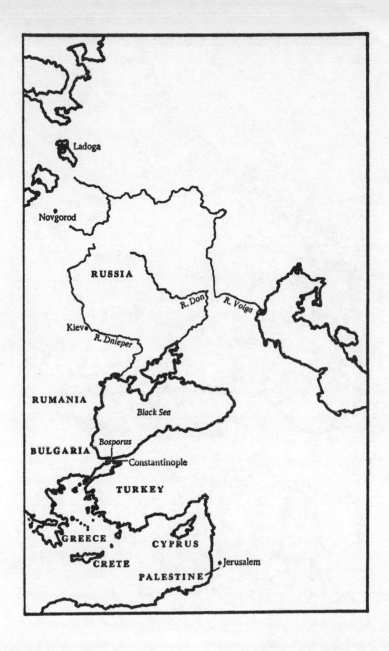